D0200814

JESUS
IN
HIS HOMELAND

BY SHERMAN E. JOHNSON

Dean of the Church Divinity School

of the Pacific

BERKELEY, CALIFORNIA

CHARLES SCRIBNER'S SONS

New York

ACKNOWLEDGEMENTS

The photographs between pages 6 and 7 came from the following sources:

THE MATSON PHOTO SERVICE, LOS ANGELES—*Fisherman of
Galilee, Mt. Hermon and the Sea of Galilee, Nazareth,
the Sea of Galilee from Hattin, and Drawing in a drag-net*

JAMES B. PRITCHARD—*Excavation of New Testament
Jericho, and New Testament Jericho*

All other photographs were supplied by the author

TO JEAN

Her ways are ways of pleasantness,
and all her paths are peace.

TABLE OF CONTENTS

LIST OF ILLUSTRATIONS

PREFACE

THIS book is a study of Jesus in the light of his geographical, cultural and religious background. My aim has been to let his commanding and unique figure emerge from this background and to determine, so far as I can, his place in the Jewish religious community. I have also tried to make some contribution toward the solution of two very difficult questions: how did hostility arise against him, and why did Christianity so quickly separate from Judaism?

I have not written a "life of Jesus," for this book does not attempt to give a full account of his teaching, nor does it deal with such important problems as the chronology of his life, his birth, his baptism, his transfiguration, or his miracles. The more modest task undertaken here is made necessary by the publication of the Dead Sea literature and other archaeological discoveries which enrich our knowledge of first-century Judaism. It seems important to deal with these new materials in such a way as to give them their proper weight while not forgetting what the scholarship of the past generation has taught us about the Pharisees and the apocalyptic literature.

J. B. Phillips in his little book, *When God Was Man* (New York, 1955), remarks that the physical and geographical background of Jesus' life is not of the highest importance. "The setting is in a sense 'accidental.' It happened in Palestine two thousand years ago, but it might

vii

just as well have been India, or South Africa, or Germany, or China, as far as the real significance is concerned. . . . It will help us far more if we study how that Man met human situations which are a permanent part of the life of mankind in all ages and in all places" (pp. 10 f.). With this I can agree in general, but I have written these studies in the conviction that, since "it happened in Palestine," the setting will sharpen the picture and more adequately show how he met his situation.

Many readers will note that instead of giving a full account of the similarities between Jesus' teaching and that of the Pharisees I have concentrated on the differences. This is not because I think the similarities insignificant; on the contrary, they are very important. But the parallels are well known, and commentaries on the gospels almost always emphasize them. The differences which are equally significant are what we have not been able to define precisely, hence my concern with them.

My interest in this group of problems goes back to my years as a student of Dr. Frederick C. Grant in the Western Theological Seminary, Evanston, Ill. To Dr. Grant and to my other teachers and colleagues in the institutions where I have learned and taught, I owe a debt that can never be repaid, though any work of mine that is worth while will be a token of my gratitude. Particular thanks are due to Professor Frank M. Cross, Jr., of the McCormick Theological Seminary, who read and criticized Chapters IV and V. The volume is dedicated to my wife. I have no words adequate to express my thanks to her for her encouragement, inspiration, counsel and love.

Like many students of the New Testament, I write as a historian who is trying to be candid and accurate, and yet I write from the perspective of the Christian tradition. I believe in the Lord who is the subject of these chapters and I also believe that he is best served if the story is told as objectively as possible. From time to time the book makes theological as well as historical judgments, and I hope that I have made clear the distinction between them. If so, the book may perhaps be useful to those who cannot agree with me theologically.

The substance of several of these chapters was given as the Reinecker Lectures at the Virginia Theological Seminary. Other parts were delivered at the School of the Prophets in San Francisco, the College of Preachers in Washington, and the Pastoral Conference of the Pacific School of Religion. Part of the substance of the last chapter was given as the first address of the Faith in Action program of NBC.

In making biblical quotations I have made my own translation except in cases where the citation is identified as coming from the Revised Standard Version of the Bible, copyright 1946 and 1952. For the Manual of Discipline I quote the translation of William H. Brownlee in *Bulletin of the American Schools of Oriented Research*, Supplementary Studies, Nos. 10-12 (New Haven, 1951), and for the Damascus Document I have used the edition of Chaim Rabin, *The Zadokite Documents* (Oxford, 1954), making my own translations.

Since I am not writing primarily for scholars, I have included only enough notes to acknowledge indebtedness for contributions of recent investigators and to provide some help for those who wish to pursue further some of the more important issues.

SHERMAN E. JOHNSON

Jerusalem
August, 1956

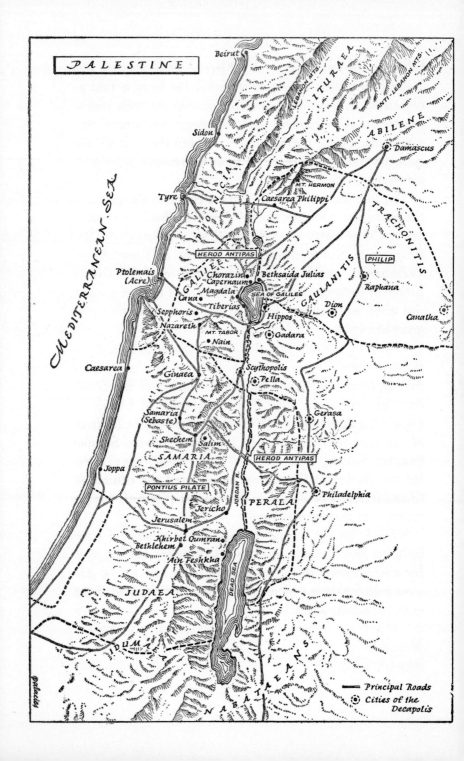

CHAPTER I

GALILEE

GALILEE, the homeland of Jesus and the site of
most of his ministry, is smaller in area than the state
of Rhode Island. It is a little larger than Wiltshire, or the
Saar territory, or the Grand Duchy of Luxembourg, about
the size of two average counties in Kansas and smaller than
Los Angeles County, California—no more than a canton in
a tiny land, for the whole of Palestine, including the
Negeb, is about the size of Vermont.

North of Jesus' homeland tower the mountains of
Lebanon. Mount Hermon, snow-capped at an elevation
of 9,100 feet, dominates the landscape to the northeast.
But Galilee is only the foothill country for the two great
ranges of Lebanon and anti-Lebanon, and lies between
them and the plain of Esdraelon—and it is a land cut up
into little rounded limestone hills, with deep valleys in
between. One large knob of hill, Mount Tabor, stands
out impressively, though it is no more than 1,843 feet high,
for it is on the edge of the plain, and its east side slopes
down steeply to the Jordan valley, and can be seen from
far below sea level. Nazareth itself lies at 1,144 feet.
Local pride has marked one of its cliffs, which drops off to
the Esdraelon plain, as the spot where the angry villagers
wished to cast Jesus down (Luke 4:29).

Bounded by the mountains on the north and the plains
on the coastal side and the south, Galilee had a fourth
natural limit, the deep rift of the Jordan, which falls
from 7 feet above sea level at Lake Huleh to 685 feet
below at the Sea of Galilee. Thus Galilee has the geological

variety which marks all Palestine as a natural wonder. Near Nazareth one can see rich red earth, colored like some of the Appalachian piedmont; a less fertile gray soil that nevertheless includes good valleys; and the disintegrated basalt around the Sea of Galilee that produced fabulous crops. Josephus called this last region the ambition of nature. But the ridges were hard, bony and unyielding, as full of rocks and boulders as a poor New England pasture. Travelers find with delight that they can easily distinguish the various soils of the parable of the Sower.

Certain parts of the California coast have the same annual rainfall as Nazareth, about 24 inches, most of it in the late autumn, winter and early spring, and the two places can produce similar plants. But Nazareth has greater extremes of heat and cold, varying from freezing weather to temperatures above 100 degrees Fahrenheit. Around the Sea of Galilee the climate is almost tropical; in the summer hot and stifling, but pleasant in winter. While the air of the hill country is bracing, its winters were none too easy for the poorly housed peasant, and it is often warmer outdoors than inside.

Many of the farmers of Jesus' day must have been small freeholders who gained a subsistence, and not much more, from the soil. Eusebius, the first great Christian historian, who wrote in the fourth century, tells of grandsons of Jude, the brother of the Lord, who had 9,000 denarii—presumably in cash—and 39 plethra of land (about 25 acres) which they worked themselves and from which they paid their taxes. We know, too, of tenant farmers who worked on a sharecropping basis for large landowners who operated estates in Galilee and other parts of Palestine at the same time. Galilee had many more forest lands than at present, covered with oaks, terebinths, carobs, laurel and other trees. Anyone might pasture his flocks in the woods—even Judaeans sometimes did so—but there was no planned forestry, and the goats must have consumed many young saplings.

Cities and villages had been built here and there, some Jewish and others pagan. Artisans and small merchants made up most of the city population. The capital had its small court and bureaucracy, and along the Sea of Galilee were fishing towns where men like Zebedee drew drag-nets or cast purse-shaped *amphiblestra*. The most important fishery, Taricheae (which may be the Magdala of the gospels), exported salted and pickled fish to all parts of the empire.

Galilee had its beautiful aspects—the rich red earth, the stone villages with their roofs of rolled mud laid on thorny branches over beams, the Galilean lake like a blue jewel set in dusky silver, the scarlet anemones that rivalled Solomon's glory, and the round top of Tabor. But it would be wrong to think of it as idyllic. Its outdoor life made it a friendlier land than northern Europe or New England, but it always knew poverty and seldom peace. It was as fiercely loved and coveted by first-century Jews as by their twentieth-century successors or by Greeks, crusaders and desert Arabs in the centuries between. The information about Galilee's climate and topography is well known; the fact of its miseries is often forgotten.

Part of its misfortune was that, being situated on the land-bridge from Africa to Asia and Europe, it was of strategic importance. The main road from Egypt to Damascus passed, in ancient times, through the plain of Esdraelon. One branch of it came just south of Mount

Tabor and across the Gennesaret plain, while the other branch went east of the Sea of Galilee. As early as 218 B.C., in the time of Antiochus III, a garrison looked down on this road from the heights of Tabor, and at least until the time of the Jewish War this and most of the other important Galilean hills were vigilant military outposts. When the Maccabees had their brief century of pride and power, it was a cardinal point in their policy to colonize Galilee with Jews. Pompey the Great, who came next, took pains to organize a synedrion or council at Sepphoris, the capital city just five miles from Nazareth. Young Herod, given his first taste of empire by his father Antipater, won his reputation as a governor of Galilee. Here, too, he secured his future power. After the Roman senate had appointed him king, he had to deal with the last of the Maccabees. Antigonus Mattathiah had been placed on the throne by the Parthians in their lightning invasion of the west, and on the plain of Arbela, just a little north of Tabor, Herod defeated him decisively.

The Gospel of Luke tells us that at the age of twelve, just when he was taking a man's place in the synagogue, Jesus with his parents visited Jerusalem and spent some time in his Father's house debating with the rabbis. If we reckon the date of his birth at about 6 B.C., two years before the death of Herod, it was when Jesus was twelve years old that Judas the Gaulonite led the revolt in Galilee against the Roman census.[1] One pictures the small band of Jewish pilgrims, as they traveled in caravan to Jerusalem, holding themselves aloof from the insurrection, yet wondering what new troubles might come upon their

---

[1] On the basis of Josephus *Ant.* xvii. 10.5; *B. J.* ii. 4.1, it is sometimes thought that Judas' rebellion began immediately after the death of Herod the Great; however, according to *Ant.* xviii. 1.1; *B. J.* ii. 8.1, Judas led a revolt about A.D. 6.

homeland. Some of Jesus' neighbors may have sympathized with Judas. But Rome could not tolerate this or any threat to its power. If the empire was to pacify the Arab tribes to the east and the southeast and secure the trade routes, and to hold Syria and all the land west of the Euphrates as a bulwark against the Parthian danger, Galilee must be under control. In the days of Jesus' ministry a great deal depended upon the political wisdom of Herod Antipas, son of Herod the Great and "tetrarch" or prince of Galilee, in governing a mixed population which included many fanatical Jewish nationalists.

Travelers who visit the Near East today often fall under its spell and long to return. The endless variety of religion, culture and language constitutes part of this undeniable charm. But although it is a fascinating ethnographic museum, the world pays a high price for it, for behind the picturesqueness lie old hatreds and rivalries that can be quickly revived and manipulated by those who play the game of power politics. The eastern Mediterranean, from Hellenistic times on, was already a cultural and linguistic mosaic. Many regions, such as proconsular Asia, hailed the coming of the Romans with enthusiasm, partook of the prosperity of their empire, and could be regarded as solid and safe. But Palestine fitted uneasily into the imperial scheme and was already as fragmented as the Balkan peninsula in the days of the Ottoman empire, both because of physical geography and the political situation.

Galilee and its neighbors were in no way homogeneous. East of Galilee lay Pella, Gadara and the other pagan cities of the Decapolis. The Jewish yoke, imposed upon them by the Maccabees, they resented bitterly, and they welcomed the Romans as deliverers. Gadara suggests swine to the modern reader of the Bible, but an ancient was

more likely to think of it as the home of the erotic poet
Meleager. A proud center of Greek culture such as this
felt keenly its superiority to the Semitic speaking people
all around; its inhabitants were colonials of the great
empire, the others were natives.

The Galilean Jew looked at it otherwise. He saw his
homeland surrounded by alien cities—Ptolemais on the
west; Tyre, Sidon and Damascus on the north; the Decapolis on the east and southeast; and, to the south, Herod's
Greek city of Sebaste in the midst of the unfriendly
Samaritans who stood as a barrier between the Galilean
and his Judaean allies. In Galilee itself there were heathen
municipalities. Heathen Sepphoris was the capital of
Galilee in Jesus' boyhood, and a decade later the government was moved to Tiberias—an unclean city because the
site was partly on a cemetery. It was only later that Jews
in any large number inhabited the place.

The tides of east and west have alternately flowed over
Palestine. The Herodian dynasty did much to foster
western culture, and the results of its efforts were not
altogether unlike those of the Crusades and the British
mandate. Cities took on the external appearances of
western civilization; the spirit of the people was altered but
little. Caesarea, Sebaste and Tiberias were monuments to
Roman power and material culture, as their very names
suggest. Roman roads and aqueducts crisscrossed the
country. The imposing remains of Gerasa and the Herodian
masonry of Hebron and Jerusalem indicate the magnifi-
cence and cost of these public works. But under the
Greek veneer were Jewish monotheism and the older Syrian
paganism. Eusebius wrote his *Onomasticon*—a gazeteer of
place names in the Bible—in the fourth century A.D., and

FISHERMAN OF GALILEE THROWING HIS NET NEAR CAPERNAUM

MT. HERMON AND THE
SEA OF GALILEE

SITE OF NEW TESTAMENT
JERICHO. VIEW TOWARD
JORDAN RIVER

ABOVE, EXCAVATION
OF NEW TESTAMENT
JERICHO

AT THE LEFT, RUINS
OF QUMRAN, SHOWI
ROOMS IN THE
MONASTERY; FERTILE
AREA OF AIN FESHKH
AND THE DEAD SEA
IN BACKGROUND

"TOWER OF DAVID" AT THE JAFFA GATE; LOWER COURSES OF MASONRY PROBABLY BELONG TO ONE OF HEROD'S TOWERS

BELOW, NEW TESTAMENT JERICHO: CIVIC CENTER OF HEROD THE GREAT OR ARCHELAUS, SHOWING ROMAN BRICK AND *opus reticulatum*

NAZARETH FROM
SOUTHEAST

SEA OF GALILEE FROM
HATTIN.
MT. OF BEATITUDES.
TELEPHOTO SHOWING
NORTH SHORE OF
THE SEA

DRAWING IN A DRAG-NET ON THE SEA OF GALILEE ON BETHSAIDA SHORE

it is remarkable that even then the pattern had changed so little—a Jewish village here, a pagan one there.

Jesus' homeland was, in fact, relatively new as a Jewish territory. Its name, "Galilee," means "circle" or "region," and its full Old Testament designation was "circle of the Gentiles." Up to the time of the Maccabees few Jews had lived there. The excavations at Sepphoris reveal no settlement on that spot before the Hellenistic period. If earlier houses had existed and were levelled off for the new construction, they must have been meagre. Aristobulus and Alexander Jannaeus, Jewish kings of the Maccabean dynasty, colonized the region with families from Jerusalem some time in the period between 104 and 75 B.C. It is even possible that some pagans in Galilee had been forced by military action to adopt Judaism. Alexander Jannaeus certainly used the sword to make Jews out of the Idumaeans of southern Judea and the Ituraeans of the northeast; but our sources are silent as regards the Galileans.

Since the boyhood home of Jesus was of this character, into what kind of Jewish life was he nurtured? The question is important because of his later conflict with the authorities. The gospels tell us very little that is specific, but they give some clear impressions. From the infancy stories of Luke one gathers that the family had a simple and genuine devotion to the ancestral religion. The parents of John the Baptist, who are closely connected with the story, were "both righteous before God, walking in all the commandments and judgments of the Lord blameless" (Luke 1:6). These chapters of Luke are permeated with quiet hope; the ancient Symeon, for example, is one who "expected the consolation of Israel" (2:25). It is tempting to think that the hymns usually called *Benedictus* (1:68-

79), *Magnificat* (1:46-55), and *Nunc Dimittis* (2:29-32)
were sung in the circles out of which Jesus came. If so, he
was born into an atmosphere of Messianic expectation.
These ancient Jews believed in a thorough revolution, soon
to arrive, in which the mighty would be hurled down from
their high privileges and their places taken by the humble
and meek of the land. We know that hymns of this sort,
which are variations on themes found in the Old Testament
Psalms, were sung by sectarian Jews, for a collection of
them has been found among the Dead Sea Scrolls. The
so-called Psalms of Solomon, preserved to us in a Greek
translation, resemble the canticles of Luke even more
closely. The Psalms of Solomon may have been written
by Pharisees or by a group like that which produced the
Dead Sea manuscripts. And, since the Dead Sea group
and John the Baptist have some characteristics in common,
and the hymns in Luke are connected nearly as much with
John as with Jesus, it may well be that the background
in which Jesus grew up was influenced by some party or
sect other than the Pharisees.

If more were known about the history of Christianity
in Galilee after the Crucifixion, there might be more light
on the background of Jesus' ministry. But the sources tell
us very little. If we assume—as perhaps we may or may
not—that Galilean Christians transmitted the materials in
the gospels which mention Galilee or whose scene is laid
in that region, then Galilee is above all the place where
men recalled Jesus' teaching about the Kingdom of God.
It is also the locality to which his Galilean followers
expected him to return in glory. Eusebius hands down
from an earlier writer, Hegesippus, some further traditions
about members of the Lord's family. There is the story,
previously mentioned, of the grandsons of Jude, who were

said to have been brought before the emperor Domitian. These men, who were suspect because they were descendants of David, disclaimed any thought of a messianic revolution on earth; the kingdom they looked for was heavenly. There is also the account of the martyrdom of James the brother of the Lord, told not only by Hegesippus but by Josephus. James seems to have the character of a quiet ascetic who fasts and prays and is withdrawn from many of the ordinary concerns of life. In the Book of Acts and the letters of Paul he is pictured as friendly to the Pharisees. From these sparse notices one might guess that later Galilean Christians continued to look for God's deliverance of Israel, but there is nothing to indicate that they were as radical as their Master. Devoted they were, beyond any doubt, but not adventurous.

CHAPTER II

THE PHARISEES

NEARLY everyone who writes on the religious situation in first-century Palestine makes his point of departure the remark of Josephus that there were four "philosophies" in Judaism. Josephus had been a general in the Jewish army in the first great revolt of A.D. 66-70. After winning some battles in Galilee early in the war, he saw the tide running strongly against his own people and became convinced, so he said, that the war would be suicidal. Accordingly he transferred his allegiance to the Romans and saw the end of the war from the other side. Later in life, while living in Rome, he wrote not only an account of the war and an autobiography, but also a defense of Judaism and a history of the *Antiquities of the Jews*, partly from a desire to interpret his people to themselves and to the Gentiles. He was born into a priestly family and claimed to be a Pharisee, but in his youth he had had enough religious curiosity to study the beliefs of other parties and to live for a time with a hermit in the Jordan valley.

It seems strange that he should describe the religious parties of Judaism as "philosophies." But he was writing for Greeks and Romans and tried to use terms that might be suggestive to them. After all, the Jewish religion looked to Greeks somewhat like a philosophical school. It fostered study, the reading of sacred books, the singing of hymns, and prayer, as some Greek philosophies did. Jews worshipped no images, and carried on sacrifice only in Jerusalem. Therefore Josephus could, with some plausibility, describe the different forms of Judaism as varying philosophies within one religious culture.

In Judaism there were, of course, more than four groups. Eusebius mentions Masbothaeans, Hemerobaptists ("daily immersers"), Galileans and others. But Josephus' four philosophies were the principal ones.

These were the Pharisees, the Sadducees, the Essenes, and the revolutionists. The last two will be discussed in later chapters. The Sadducees need concern us only briefly. We know little about them, and that little comes mainly from the prejudiced writings of their opponents. Their strength came mainly from a small group of wealthy priestly families in Jerusalem, and from these were chosen most, if not all, of the high priests during that part of the first century A.D. when Rome ruled Judaea through procurators. The Sadducees are known to have existed as a separate group at least as far back as the time of John Hyrcanus (135-105 B.C.). There is some reason to think that the early Sadducees in Maccabean times went far to compromise with the paganism of their Syrian overlords; and in the time of Jesus such Sadducees as Annas and Caiaphas seemed more intent on their own privileges and on collaboration with the Roman government than on any positive religious leadership according to the spirit of the Old Testament.

According to Pharisaic testimony, the Sadducees had a lower standard of education and piety than that of the Pharisees. They may have represented for the most part the conservative, wealthy, land-owning element among the priests; they resisted innovations, such as the doctrine of the resurrection; and they stood on the letter of the Bible and their own tradition. If there were good Sadducees— and it is hard to think that there were not—perhaps their prototype was Yeshua ben Sira, author of the book called Ecclesiasticus in the English Apocrypha. Yeshua combines a reverence for the high priesthood with real piety, and sound, though conservative, common sense.

Of all the first-century Jewish groups, the Pharisees are best known to us. Beside what Josephus tells us, we have the contemporary testimony of the New Testament, which is usually unfavorable, and, finally, the vast body of rabbinic literature—the Mishnah, in which the oral law was first codified, the other parts of the Talmud, the Midrashim or commentaries on the Bible—all of which comes out of the Pharisaic tradition. Of one thing there can be no doubt: the Pharisees included the finest minds and represented the most lively intellectual activity in Judaism. They appear to be truer to the spirit of the Old Testament than either Sadducees or Essenes. At least they were in the main stream of the legal tradition of the Hebrew Bible, and they were not unconscious of the prophets, though they always read them in the light of the Law. In contrast to the other parties, they had a more realistic and responsible outlook toward the everyday problems of the people, and they made a sincere and constant effort to adapt the religious Law to the conditions of the age so that it might guide man in all his dealings. To the Pharisees the Old Testament Law was perfect and permanent. If some of its provisions seemed antiquated and impossible to apply, one had only to look for the true interpretation. The Pharisees believed that they could find this either through an ingenious study of scripture itself or in the oral tradition handed down by rabbis or teachers of their party.

Among the Pharisees of the early first century there

were two principal schools of thought. One was headed by the liberal, innovating Rabbi Hillel, who came originally from Babylonia; the other led by the Palestinian Rabbi Shammai, who was more traditional in his rulings and is sometimes thought to have been more in touch with the ideas of the agricultural population than Hillel, the city man.

Since Judaism was a religious Law and presupposed a theocratic state, there was no clear line drawn between religious and ordinary civil and criminal provisions of the Law. Just as in Old Testament times, all Jewish law was religious law. The Roman authorities did not interfere with local law except when they thought it necessary. If we would assess the contribution of the Pharisees fairly, we must remember that their scribes were not just canon lawyers but that they constituted the national bar and judiciary, and we must take into consideration the background of their rulings.

For example, it is true that, according to Hillel, a man could divorce his wife for any cause, while Shammai restricted the cause to unchastity or at least gross immodesty. It is also true that a woman could not divorce her husband. On the other hand, the rabbis held that a man must divorce his wife in proper legal form and could not afterward retract his action without her consent; the woman was free. Futhermore, under certain circumstances a woman could go before the court and force her husband to divorce her. This marked a stage forward in the protection of women.

Many Pharisaic legal rulings benefited the common man. One example is the *prosbul* devised by Hillel, which circumvented the Old Testament law requiring that debts

be forgiven in the sabbatical year. This enabled poor
people to obtain loans at a time when otherwise no creditor
would be willing to lend.

All of this indicates that the first-century Pharisee had
a considerable sense of social responsibility. Perhaps it is
roughly accurate to say that the Pharisees tried to adapt
the Law to existing circumstances; the Sadducees refused
to face new problems and held that where the Bible made
no provision there was no law; while the Essenes, who
withdrew as far as possible from the society around them,
attempted to found an ideal community where a rigorous
law could be kept.

What we would call the specifically *religious* ideas of
the Pharisees were also an advance on the past. Like Jesus,
the Pharisees believed in the resurrection. They held that
sacrifices and the Day of Atonement were limited in their
efficacy to remove guilt, and insisted that repentance and
restitution were the only remedy for sins against the
moral law. The demand for repentance, forgiveness, mercy,
and outgoing lovingkindness appears all through the
rabbinic writings which go back to the Pharisaic movement.

The Pharisees thought of all life as brought under God's
revelation. His Law had an answer for every human
problem that could arise. Therefore they took upon themselves the heroic task of educating the entire nation in
its religion; and they took seriously the teaching of
Leviticus that all of Israel was a people intended to be
holy and set apart to the Lord. Every person was capable
of learning the law that applied to him and acting upon
it. If it was good for a priest to be holy in the technical
sense of ceremonial purity, it was certainly appropriate for
dedicated laymen to observe the same laws of cleanliness.

Through much of its history, Judaism has been a far-reaching force for education and religious democracy.

The Pharisaic movement apparently began among *haburoth*, groups of associates or *haburim* who banded themselves together to observe the Law. These groups attracted others to themselves and made their influence felt in government, in the courts, and in community life generally. Their leaders were rabbis or experts in the Law. Because of their learning their opinions came increasingly to be enforced by local courts and by the Great Sanhedrin in Jerusalem.

The theocratic ideal of education and social control required positive guidance of the religious life of the people. The Pharisees are among the world's great spiritual directors. Whenever possible they built a fence about the Law "to keep a man far from transgression." Not only the evil act itself was prohibited but other seemingly harmless acts which might lead toward the sin. The same principle was applied to mitigate cruelty so far as possible. If Deut. 25:3 set the limit of corporal punishment at forty lashes, the Pharisees reduced it to thirty-nine lest the count be accidentally exceeded. To say that the court should not have inflicted whipping at all would be to judge ancient people by our own recently adopted standards. The whole purpose of the hedge about the Law is the restriction of liberty for the sake of security and protection. The principle is that which provides play pens for children and safety zones on city streets.

This concentration on the Law subtly reduced the importance of the Temple, the priesthood and other religious institutions. Worship, fasts and festivals were all part of the Law, and important chiefly because they were commandments of God. At the same time, the Pharisees emphasized the value of prayer, communion with God, and works of love and mercy. God had commanded these. A man might, in fact, go beyond what the Law strictly commanded, and this was regarded as praiseworthy.

Pharisaism was a zealous missionary movement. Its purpose was to restore the religious life of the nation and bring it into conformity with what the Pharisees understood to be God's revealed will. The mission extended to Gentiles as well. The success of this movement is shown by the fact that after the second Jewish revolt (A.D. 132-135) all other religious parties disappeared.

Jesus certainly entered into controversy with the Pharisees. In many things, of course, he agreed with them. The striking parallels to his sayings which are found scattered all through the rabbinic literature bear witness that he and they both come out of the main stream of Judaism and are descendants of the lawgivers, the prophets and the Psalmists. Yet there were far-reaching and bitter differences. An attempt to see Jesus against the background of his environment leads one to ask how the differences can be accurately defined and what were the principles and motives behind them. Granting that he transcended his own background, as every creative religious teacher and prophet must to some degree do, it is still true that a new religious movement always has its setting in the culture around it. Jesus came out of Galilee, and there is some slight evidence that a Galilean party or point of view existed in the Jewish religious world. He must have been conscious of this. What was his relation to the other Galileans? And, against this background, what can we make of his opposition to the Pharisees?

· CHAPTER III ·

JESUS AND THE GALILEANS

JESUS began his ministry about the year A.D. 28. Twenty-two years had passed since the revolt against the census led by Judas the Gaulonite, and the accession of Herod Antipas as tetrarch. Ever since Antipas' father, Herod the Great, had become King of the Jews, Roman power and culture had progressively influenced Palestinian life. How profound the social changes had been it is difficult to say, but one response to the cultural challenge of the west was the rebellious nationalistic spirit which, more than elsewhere, flared in Galilee. The other response was the successful attempt of the Pharisees to strengthen the religious and cultural power of Judaism. This also had its effect on Galilee.

Just about the time of Jesus' ministry, the Pharisees were beginning their great infiltration, which was destined to make Tiberias the Pharisaic capital and Galilee the center of Palestinian Judaism in the second and third centuries. Our evidence for this statement rests partly on the gospels, which portray Jesus' opponents as Pharisaic scribes from Jerusalem.

In Galilee the Pharisees came into collision with other groups. This we know because the Talmud contains remarks on the ʿamme ha-ares of Galilee, the legal peculiarities which prevailed there, and the boorishness of some rabbis—Pharisees though they were—who came from that region. Galilee was evidently a mission field for the Pharisees, and here, if a Galilean religious party existed, the Pharisees met them. Eusebius mentions such a group,

17

and President Louis Finkelstein, of the Jewish Theological
Seminary in New York, has collected evidence to show that
the Galilean Jews were not originally Pharisees.[1]

In Galilee were many people whom the Talmud calls
'amme ha-ares. This Hebrew phrase is a curious plural of
the collective noun *'am ha-ares*, "people of the land." The
term seems to mean "country people," but the Pharisees
apparently used it technically to refer to those who had
no religious learning in the Pharisaic sense of the word or
were actually illiterate. Finkelstein argues that many of the
large landowners who dominated Galilee belonged to this
group. From the Pharisees' point of view they were practically unchurched. They may have observed some religious
customs but only those handed down by their forefathers.
Some of them no doubt deserved the criticism made of
them and were Jews only in name.

There were Pharisees in Galilee, but again Finkelstein's
evidence suggests that they belonged to the school of
Shammai, the more conservative and agrarian-minded
rabbi, whose influence was finally eclipsed by that of Hillel.

Many of the upper-class people of Galilee were violent
nationalists. The middle classes, made up of small landowners and the artisans and traders of the towns, were
even more ardent zealots, and some of them were adherents
of religious parties opposed to the Pharisees. The Galileans
differed from the Jews of Jerusalem in their pugnacity, the
dialect of Aramaic which they spoke, and in many of their
secular and religious customs: they were, for the most
part, either non-Pharisaic or anti-Pharisaic.

When we go further and try to define the position of
the Galilean party, we have only a few small pieces of
evidence.

[1] L. Finkelstein, *The Pharisees* (Philadelphia, 1938), I, pp. 40-60.

Dr. Julian Morgenstern some years ago developed a theory that Jesus and other Galilean Jews did not keep the Passover on the same day as the Jews of Jerusalem. It is a curious and baffling fact that, according to Mark, Jesus' last supper was a Passover, while in the Gospel of John Jesus dies on the Cross about the time when the paschal lambs would be slain, and the Passover is not eaten until that night. The Jewish day begins at sunset. On Mark's reckoning, then, the Last Supper and Crucifixion would seem to take place on the fifteenth day of the Jewish month Nisan, but according to John on the fourteenth. Morgenstern suggests that the Galileans followed strictly the procedure of Exod. 12:1-14 and ate the Passover at the beginning of the fourteenth of Nisan, while the Jews of Jerusalem followed what has since been the universal Jewish custom and ate it on the fifteenth.[2] On Morgenstern's assumption, both Mark and John are correct: Jesus' Last Supper was a Passover, but held one day before the Jerusalem festival. If this theory is correct, it would seem to show that the Galileans were more conservative, more dependent on the letter of the Bible for their ceremonial tradition, than the Pharisees.

We do know that the Pharisees criticized the Galileans for serving milk with meat. The Old Testament prohibits boiling a kid in its mother's milk (Exod. 23:19; Deut. 14:21), and quite understandably, because as we know from the Ras Shamra texts of about 1500 B.C., this was a practice of Syrian paganism. The Pharisees, in building their fence about the Law, went further and forbade eating any meat and any dairy products at the same meal—a rule

---

[2] Dr. Morgenstern has not yet published on this subject but permitted me to include a reference to his theory in *The Interpreter's Bible*, VII (New York, 1951), p. 572.

still observed by orthodox Jews. The Galileans kept the Old Testament law but not the Pharisaic expansion.

Such conservatism may well have been characteristic of Palestinian farmers, particularly in out-of-the-way places like Galilee which were far from Jerusalem. We know further that most peasants—whether in Galilee or else-where—resisted the rule of the second tithe and the extension of tithing to vegetables and herbs. The Old Testament tithe laws were conflicting and difficult to interpret. Although they probably contemplated only a single tithe or tenth, the Pharisees interpreted them as referring to two tithes. The first was to be paid to the priests. The second tithe had to be consumed by the farmer and his family in Jerusalem. The Old Testament provisions for the first tithe were vague and may not originally have intended more than a tithe on grain, oil and wine. Both of these Pharisaic rulings were costly to farmers, particularly since secular taxes were also assessed. The school of Hillel—but not the more agrarian-minded school of Shammai—went so far as to declare all Galilean olive oil impure because it was so difficult to answer with certainty the question whether tithes on it had been paid.

Jesus and his disciples were criticized for plucking grain on the Sabbath (Mark 2:23-24). Finkelstein compares this with the situation at Jericho, where the residents did not dare to violate the Law as openly as this, but neverthe-less flouted Pharisaic rulings by eating fruit which had fallen from the trees on the Sabbath.

Certainly Jesus' rulings at some points agree with the Galileans against the Pharisees. The question, however, is whether his attitude is Galilean or agrarian or sectarian, or whether it rests on other foundations. The answer is to be found in certain sayings groups and stories in the synoptic gospels, many of which have their setting in Galilee.

We have already mentioned the issues of tithing and plucking of grain on the Sabbath. It is easy to imagine the attitude of the Galilean peasant. He may not have been influenced by any profound religious motive at all; he was simply a practical man who saw no reason to alter his immemorial customs at the demand of scholars from the city. Rabbi Akiba, who lived in the late first and early second centuries of our era, and became one of the saints of Judaism, once told his students, "When I was an 'am ha-ares, I used to say that if I could get hold of one of those scholars I would bite him like an ass." The students corrected him: "You mean, like a dog." "No," said Akiba, "an ass's bite breaks bones."

We do not find in Jesus' teaching any hostility to scholarship as such. Though he denounces rabbis who load people with grievous burdens and take away the key of knowledge (Luke 11:46, 52=Matt. 23:4, 13), our sources find him praising an occasional rabbi or lawyer (Mark 12:34). Jesus does not reject the Jerusalem scholars because they are scholars, nor does he rest his case on tradition. His criticism is that the Pharisees, while zealous at tithing, neglect justice and the love of God (Luke 11:42; or, as Matt. 23:23 has it, "justice, mercy and faith"). When he discusses the plucking of grain on the Sabbath (Mark 2:23-38), he appeals to the sensible example of David, who, when he was hungry, ate the loaves presented to God. The precedent is set by one of the great heroes of the Bible rather than by Palestinian custom or some other tradition. The kernel of the story is in the words, "The Sabbath came into being for the sake of man, and not man for the sake of the Sabbath" (2:27). The saying has a parallel in rabbinic literature but Jesus uses it as a radical criticism of the current exposition of the Sabbath law. Jesus sympathized with his neighbors in certain matters of controversy, but these sayings do not betray a particularly Galilean or agrarian point of view. There is no sufficient evidence, then, that Jesus was a "Galilean" party man.

CHAPTER IV

THE ESSENES AND EARLY CHRISTIANITY

JESUS was not a member of a Galilean party, nor was he a Pharisee or Sadducee. Could he have been influenced by some other Jewish party? In the past hundred years, more than one scholar, searching for the point of contact between Jesus and his environment, has suggested that he derived some of his ideas and practices from the Essenes. Recent manuscript discoveries—the most dramatic in modern times—have opened the question again.

The Essenes were a sect or religious order that lived in the cities of Judah and in the Jordan valley near the Dead Sea in the centuries just before the beginning of our era. Until recent years, almost our only knowledge of them came from the Jewish historian Josephus, from Philo the Jewish philosopher, and from the Roman writer Pliny—all of whom lived in the first century A.D. To these writers, as to later students, they were a great curiosity, and what is said about them indicates that they were in many ways apart from average Judaism.

Four thousand of the Essenes, according to Josephus, were celibate and lived in a kind of monastic community. Others, who married, did so only for the purpose of procreating children. Since most Jews held that marriage and family life were a blessing and a commandment of God, this celibacy is, to say the least, something new in Judaism.

Like later monastic orders, the Essenes owned their

possessions in common and had a special garb—in this case white. They kept silence in the morning except for prayers, worked in the fields during the afternoon, and had priestly blessings before their two meals, which they ate at midday and in the evening. Certain officers had authority over them and in what might be called the chapter meeting the members took turns speaking in a regularly fixed order. A man could not enter the community except after a year's probation and then he had to take binding vows. These had to do with obligations to the community and to people outside, and included a promise to keep secret the special doctrines and books of the order. One indication of their asceticism was that they took cold baths and did not anoint their bodies with oil. In performing natural functions they followed methods of sanitation set forth in the rule of Deut. 23:12-14 regarding conduct in a holy war.

Josephus makes a puzzling statement about their sacrificial customs. He says that they offered no sacrifices in the Jerusalem Temple, for they had purer offerings of their own; and yet, he adds, they sent offerings to the Temple. According to Josephus, they taught that the soul was immortal. Perhaps this means that the Essenes rejected the Pharisaic doctrine of the resurrection of the body, but it may be that Josephus is simply translating "resurrection" into Greek terms. Fate (by which Josephus probably means predestination) they declared to be the master of all things; nothing happens to man without its decree. Like Jesus they seem to have forbidden the taking of oaths; to do so was worse than perjury. They vowed to exercise piety and justice, to do no harm to others, and to hate the wicked and help the righteous.

Apart from some of their more unusual practices, the Essenes resemble some of the Pharisaic brotherhoods of the first century, though they were more strict. It is possible, as a few scholars suggest, that both Pharisees and Essenes developed out of the *hasidim*, who, in the Maccabean period, when Judaism was in danger of being swallowed up by pagan culture, bound themselves to keep the Law more rigorously.

In the light of all this, it has been remarked that Jesus never married, and that while St. Paul held marriage to be lawful and right, he advised his followers to remain single if they could do so. No women were present at the Last Supper, though this may have no significance other than Near Eastern custom. The Christian church in Jerusalem at one time practiced communal ownership; how extensively, we do not know. It is not recorded that Jesus took part in temple worship or that, before the resurrection, his followers did so. Both the Gospel of Matthew and the Epistle of James forbid oaths. Jesus, like the Essenes, taught his people not to lord it over one another. Those who look for similarities between the Essenes and the early Christians underline these facts, but beyond them there is very little in Josephus' account of Essenism that suggests primitive Christianity.

Until recently no one would have guessed that we might ever have further information about this obscure group; after all, they were a secret order and our information about them came from outsiders. Nor were we hopeful of filling in the jigsaw puzzle that constitutes early sectarian Judaism, for the vast body of Jewish literature previously known is derived from the Pharisees, though it was known that prophets, hermits and baptist groups lived in the Jordan valley. One piece of the puzzle came to light in 1910, when Solomon Schechter published fragments of two manuscripts belonging to the tenth century

A.D. or later.[1] These were found in an old Cairo synagogue, in the *genizah* where discarded manuscripts were
stored, together with some writings of the Karaite sect
which seems to have arisen no earlier than the eighth
century of our era.

Some scholars thought that the original documents,
of which these manuscripts were copies, had been written
about the time of the birth of Jesus, but it was impossible
to be certain. The sect which produced them bitterly
rejected the Jerusalem priesthood. It proclaimed a new
covenant "in the land of Damascus," considered its own
priests to be the only true sons of Zadok, who had been
Solomon's chief priest, and looked for a Messiah or
Messiahs "from Aaron and Israel." Its laws were stricter
than those of the Pharisees. At one or two points there were
apparent similarities to Jesus' teaching.

Thirty-seven years passed before more parts of the
puzzle came to light. Then one day bedouin Arabs of the
Ta'amireh tribe, who live near the north end of the Dead
Sea, discovered a cave and in it jars containing ancient
scrolls written on leather. In the course of time part of the
manuscripts came into the possession of the Syrian Orthodox Archbishop in Jerusalem and others were purchased
by the Hebrew University. More recently the Syrian
Archbishop's manuscripts have been sold and given to the
state of Israel, so that the larger manuscripts of the
original find—or at least those that have come to light—
are now in the Jewish part of Jerusalem.

The Archbishop acquired an almost complete copy of
the biblical book of Isaiah, a commentary or midrash on
the first two chapters of Habakkuk composed by a sect

[1] S. Schechter, *Fragments of a Zadokite Work* (Cambridge, 1910). More
recent editions are L. Rost, *Die Damaskusschrift,* "Kleine Texte," No. 167
(Berlin, 1933), and C. Rabin, *The Zadokite Documents* (Oxford, 1954).

which is probably identical with the "Zadokite" or "Damascus" group, a Manual of Discipline from the same sect, and a fourth scroll which was in such poor condition that it was doubtful whether it could be unrolled without being destroyed. It has now been identified as a paraphrase and expansion of Genesis. Among those originally bought by the Hebrew Universtiy of Jerusalem are two interesting works. One has come to be known as the War Scroll (*Milhamah*) or The War of the Sons of Light against the Sons of Darkness. This consists of ritual and tactical directions for battle in the final great holy war against the Gentiles. The other is a collection of Hymns of Thanksgiving (*Hōdâyôth*), not unlike the canticles of Luke (Luke 1:46-55; 1:68-79; 2:29-32) and the Psalms of Solomon, and expressing a profound piety.

The prevailing opinion is that these manuscripts were written not long before the beginning of the Christian era. They almost certainly come from the same Jewish group which produced Schechter's fragments, and it is almost equally certain that this is the Essene sect.

Discovery of these utterly unique manuscripts, the existence of which no one would have dared to hope for, touched off an intensive archaeological search of the whole region. The Palestine Museum, the Jordan Department of Antiquities, the École Biblique et Archéologique, the American School of Oriental Research, and the Bedouins of the neighborhood made important finds. Eleven caves yielded important collections of fragments, particularly those known as Qumran Caves One, Four, and Eleven. The material now becoming available to biblical scholars and historians overwhelms the imagination. There are parts of practically every book of the Hebrew Bible, and these fragments are of the highest importance for reconstruction of the original text. Most of these are on leather but a few are written on papyrus. Beside the Hebrew originals there are fragments of Greek translations. Equally rich are the non-biblical writings. There are other copies of documents included in those first found—the Manual of Discipline, the Thanksgiving Psalms, and the War Scroll. Parts of the Apocrypha of the English Bible—Tobit and Ecclesiasticus or Ben Sira—are also included, as well as books called Pseudepigrapha and long known in translated form in Greek, Syriac and other languages; for example, Jubilees, Enoch, and the Testament of Levi. To these are added commentaries on Isaiah, Hosea, Nahum, Micah and the Psalms, written by members of the Essene sect; a number of apocalypses giving views of the future age; other psalms, prayers and liturgical pieces; lists of courses of priests; works dealing with the calendar; collections of biblical prophecies; and parts of many other books. The small team of scholars working in the Palestine Museum in Jerusalem makes important discoveries almost every week, and bits of scrolls are still being found and brought in. Cave Three even yielded a copper scroll giving directions for the finding of tons of gold and other buried treasure.

Several miles from Khirbet Qumran is the Wady Murabba'at, where the other scroll-bearing caves have been found. The new materials from Murabba'at, which are not considered to be related to the Qumran sect, include a letter written by a Jewish military officer at the time of the revolt of Simeon bar Koziba (known to Christian sources as bar Kokhba, son of the star) in the early second century A.D. But this is another story.

Archaeologists who excavated the sect's monastery or community center at Khirbet Qumran in the neighborhood of the caves, have discovered the common refectory and several Roman cisterns, two of which might have served as baths. Nearby was found the scriptorium where manuscripts must have been copied, and in it the writing implements and the bowls in which the scribes washed their hands before entering on their sacred work, or perhaps after they had concluded it. The writing of the divine Name was believed to "defile" or "make holy" the hands and they had to wash before performing other tasks.

Several of the skeletons discovered in the Qumran cemetery are evidently those of women. A manuscript fragment consisting of two columns, recently published by Barthélemy and Milik, and belonging either to the Manual of Discipline or another law book, gives explicit rules about marriage. This is positive evidence, however slight, that there were women in the community, and it appears that not all of the Qumran Essenes were celibates.

One has to imagine them as a group of Jewish farmers who held themselves aloof from other less holy Israelites and perhaps tilled fields in the sub-tropical lower Jordan valley. The abundant spring of 'Ain Feshkha, near Khirbet Qumran, would have provided water for the crops of the monastery itself. Irrigation was practiced extensively in some parts of Palestine in the Roman period, and if this was the case at the north end of the Dead Sea the land could have supported many more people than today. Particularly in times of war and persecution, the sectaries fled to caves to preserve their lives and their sacred books. Evidence from coins found in the excavation of the monastery has suggested that an earthquake and the accession of Herod the Great (about 37 B.C.) led the members of the order to flee from their monastery and reoccupy it only after his

death (4 B.C.). Possibly they migrated to Damascus during
this period. If so, at that time they wrote the book discovered by Schechter. Many of the brothers must have been
slain at the time of the first Jewish revolt in A.D. 66-70;
there is no evidence of their having occupied Khirbet Qumran after the war. Enough of their writings survived to influence the mediaeval Karaites and other Jews. As long as
the group lasted, it was not without weight in the Jewish
world. Hard-working, self-sacrificing, stubborn and in-
transigent, they kept up such relations with other Jews as
they conscientiously could, tried to convert the well-dis-
posed, and resisted those who opposed them.

Certain it is that the Jordan valley, and the hot, dry,
rocky wilderness around the Dead Sea were the stronghold of sectarianism. Even at a later time, it was in this
region—or at least the northern part of it—that so many
Jewish Christians lived, those Ebionites or "poor" who held
to the Jewish Law after the Great Church had followed
the Apostle Paul in abrogating most of it.

This sect, whose memory has so recently been revived,
must be a significant part of the background of Jesus' life
and teaching. No Jew can have failed to know something
about the Essenes. Furthermore, the new Christian Church,
as it is portrayed in the Book of Acts, is very much like
the Qumran community. The two problems—the possible
relation between Jesus and the Essenes, and the relation
between the Essenes and the early Christians—are separate
ones, and the latter will be considered first.

The Dead Sea sect, like the early Christians, constituted a community of a New Covenant. It was related
to God, so its members believed, in a covenant of *hesed*
or loyal love. This word, sometimes translated "friend-

ship" or "mercy," is rendered as "kindness" in the Revised Standard Version of Micah 6:8:

> He has showed you, O man, what is good;
>   and what does the Lord require of you
> But to do justice, and to love kindness,
>   and to walk humbly with your God?

It is not only a covenant of love or mercy, but, as the Damascus Document says, a "new covenant." Here, as in Christian writings, the phrase undoubtedly recalls such passages as Jer. 31:33 (RSV):

> But this is the covenant which I will make with the house of Israel after those days, says the Lord: I will put my law within them, and I will write it upon their hearts; and I will be their God, and they shall be my people.

In the spirit of such a prophecy, the Dead Sea sectaries desired, as they said,

> to love everything that He has chosen, and to hate everything that He has rejected; to keep far from every evil and to cling to every good deed; and to practice truth and righteousness and justice in the land; and to walk no more in the stubbornness of a guilty heart and lustful eyes so as to do any evil (Manual of Discipline [hereafter cited as 1QS] 1:3-7).

However strange some of the provisions of the Manual, it is written by people who "wait for the consolation of Israel" and love the Old Testament prophets, and who, like the father of John the Baptist, desire to walk "in all the commandments and judgments of the Lord blameless."

Part of the Manual of Discipline seems to describe an

annual ritual for entering into the Covenant. New members may have been initiated at this time, but the rite is more than an initiation. Certain Old Testament scholars believe that at one time the Jews formally renewed their allegiance year by year, and this provision of the Manual lends strength to the theory. Such a solemn service would have had a profound psychological effect in holding the community true to its ideals. First the priests, then the Levites, and then the Israelites or Laymen affirmed their allegiance to the Covenant, and promised to keep God's commandments even though they might be persecuted. As the people entered the Covenant, the priests and Levites uttered blessings and the people responded, "Amen, amen." Then followed two sermons or solemn historical statements: the priests recounted God's mighty acts and the Levites the iniquities of Israel. After this the priests pronounced a blessing on the covenanters and the Levites a curse on "the men of Belial's lot" and the ritual concluded with a solemn curse by both priests and Levites on any who should take the covenant lightly and backslide. The people assented to all parts of the ritual by double Amens.

The Essene neophyte had to go through various degrees, so to speak, before being fully professed, and Josephus speaks of four classes of members based on their seniority in the order. The Qumran sect is certainly Essene in that it required a period of probation lasting one year. During that time the novice was not allowed to touch the "purity" of the membership, i.e. their food and drink. His property was held in trust during a second year, and he was still not allowed to share in the order's feasts. But if at the end of the second year he was found worthy, he was enrolled in the order and his goods became the property of the brotherhood.

Each man was commanded to love his brother as himself, to strengthen the poor, the needy and the stranger, and to seek his brother's well-being. Once initiated into the group the neophyte had to give his possessions into the common store, and anyone who lied about the extent of his wealth was severely punished. Here we are reminded of the story of Ananias and Sapphira in Acts 5:1-11.

There must, however, have been some private ownership in the group—at least in its Damascus community—for the Damascus Document contains laws concerning lost property, dedication of property, and contributions to the fund for the poor.

Occasionally the members of the sect describe themselves as "the poor." This is the word of honor used in the Psalms to describe the faithful Israelites who cry out to God against their rich oppressors and look to him for their vindication (Pss. 10, 12, 14). When Jesus said, "Blessed are the poor [in spirit]," he had in mind not merely the penniless but those who could say,

> My eyes are ever toward the Lord,
> for he will pluck my feet out of the net (Ps. 25:15, RSV).

Holy poverty, with its virtues and its danger of self-righteousness, was a mark of the Dead Sea community, just as later on it characterized the church in Jerusalem.

Nothing suggests that the Jerusalem church had rules for entrance as elaborate as those of the Essenes. But the two groups are similar in that baptism is closely related to the Spirit. The Qumran sectary apparently underwent a baptism after his spirit had been cleansed by repentance and obedience (1QS 3:7-9). The Manual speaks of God cleansing the members of the order through his Holy

Spirit, "sprinkling upon him a Spirit of truth as purifying water" (4:21). We are reminded of the New Testament idea of baptism in water and the Spirit, and also of Josephus' remark that John the Baptist administered his rite for the purifying of the flesh, the soul having already been cleansed by acts of righteousness (*Ant.* xviii. 5. 2). But we cannot be sure that the baptism of the Dead Sea group was a decisive rite that initiated the believer and was once-for-all. The members may have resorted to a number of ritual purifications.

The order had solemn common meals at which priests pronounced the blessings. The two-column document published by Barthélemy and Milik provides also a form for celebrating what we might call the Messianic Banquet. Both the priest and the Messiah of Israel are present, but the priest takes precedence over the Messiah, since he gives the blessing and eats first of the food. Many questions arise from this fragment. Since the Manual of Discipline and the Damascus Document speak of the Messiah or Messiahs of Aaron and Israel, does this mean that there will be two Messiahs, one a priest and one a layman? One is reminded of Joshua and Zerubbabel in the Old Testament, or of Simeon and Eleazar in the Second Revolt. Or is there but one Messiah? Although this is much less likely, in this case "Aaron and Israel" would be a term for the holy community, which contains priests and laymen.

The Messianic Banquet is a famous theme of Jewish preaching employed by both the Pharisaic rabbis and Jesus. The Jews often pictured the coming age as a great banquet in which all God's people would be fed and satisfied. With Abraham, Isaac and Jacob they would all sit at table in the Kingdom of God (Matt. 8:11). To be in Abraham's bosom means to be on his right side, at the seat of honor in the banquet (Luke 16:22). According to one imaginative conception, based on Ps. 74:14, the great sea-monster Leviathan was to be cut up and given to the people for food. One of Jesus' greatest parables pictures the Kingdom of God as a great supper (Matt. 22:1-14=Luke 14:16-24). And it is often thought that when the evangelists recorded the story of the feeding of the five thousand (Mark 6:35-44 and parallels) they thought of this as a foreshadowing of the Messianic Banquet. The banquet is a formative element in early Christian worship, notably in the Didache or Teaching of the Twelve Apostles.

The question must then be asked: is this Qumran banquet nothing more than a prophecy of something that will happen only in the coming age, or is the Messianic Banquet anticipated by a ritual meal? If the latter is the true interpretation, we have something analogous to the Christian Eucharist, which brings the events of the last days down into the present. Furthermore, the parts of the priest and the Messiah would have to be enacted by living persons.

Closely related to this is the question of the Holy War. The War Scroll contains an elaborate ritual for going into battle, with the inscriptions for the banners, the war cries and prayers, purifications and thanksgivings that are appropriate for such a combat against the Gentiles. The fragment we have been considering provides not only directions for the banquet but also for enrollment of men in the army, together with rules for marriage and other prescriptions for community life. Clearly all of this—the Holy War included—is intended to be fulfilled on this earth and at a near time.

The Manual of Discipline also requires that wherever ten men of the order live there must be a man to expound the Torah or Jewish Law, and according to the Damascus

Document this must be a priest. Not only was the Torah to be explained and preached on during the day, but all through the night three shifts of men carried on the sacred task. The many commentaries found at Qumran are evidently products of this endeavor.

This kind of biblical study was essential to the Essenes. Their New Covenant rested, as in Christianity, on the authoritative utterances of a great teacher. Although most of the practices of the Qumran sect had some basis in the Old Testament, many of the laws were new and could not claim authority in ancient tradition. Every religious group which emphasizes law rather than prophecy finds some difficulty in establishing authority for its innovations and sectarian peculiarities. Pharisaism had its own solution. It appealed to both oral traditions from the past and its own interpretation of scripture. By ingenious and—to us— forced explanations of biblical passages the Pharisees gave sanction to rulings that could not be drawn from the clear and obvious sense of the Bible.

The ingenuity of the Dead Sea sect was equally great. Its writers used scripture to defend its legal rulings but especially to discover that recent events in the life of Israel had been prophesied of old. Like the early Christians, they used proof texts. Christians regarded the prophecy of Isa. 40:3 as applying to John the Baptist: "The voice of one crying in the wilderness, Prepare ye the way of the Lord; make his paths straight." To the Essenes the same verse was a prophecy and mandate for their work; in the desert they were to prepare the way of the Lord. Both Essenes and early Christians collected *testimonia* or chains of Old Testament prophecies and used them in teaching. One of the Dead Sea manuscripts, a single sheet of leather, is particularly interesting. It begins with Deut. 5:28-29, in which God expresses to Moses the wish that his people might always stand in awe of him and keep his commandments. The next quotation is from Deut. 18:18-19, containing the promise that a prophet like Moses would be raised up from among the Hebrews. This, together with the similar passage Deut. 18:15, is used in Peter's speech (Acts 3:22-23) as a prophecy of Jesus, the second Moses. Third comes a citation of Num. 24:15-17, where Balaam prophesies that a star will arise from Jacob. Early Christians often used this prophecy of the star in connection with Jesus, and it may be referred to in Rev. 22:16 and the story of the Wise Men (Matt. 2:1-12). In the Damascus Document, of course, the "star" is the priestly Messiah. The Essene fragment continues with Deut. 33:8-11, the blessing of Moses on Levi, a valuable text for the purposes of the sect, since it claimed to have the only loyal priesthood, and Levi is the typical priestly Messiah. Finally a non-canonical book is quoted by the fragment.

In such books as Habakkuk the Qumran commentators sought hidden meanings. Even a peculiarity of spelling, or a variant text, might be significant. Words were manipulated, the consonants in them rearranged, or similar letters substituted, or a word was divided into two or more parts, in order to produce a new interpretation. More than one meaning might be attached to the same word. Pharisaic rabbis of the early centuries use many, if not all, of the same methods.

The covenanters did not claim to find all their laws in the Bible, nor apparently did they claim, as did the Pharisees, an oral tradition in unbroken succession from Moses and the prophets. The reason for their preoccupation with prophecy and its fulfilment was that they had a great lawgiver of their own. This figure is never given a name in the sources now available, nor is the story of his life told, but both the Damascus Document and the Habakkuk Commentary mention him. He is called the "Teacher of Righteousness" and it is he who must have laid down the lines on which the sect developed. According to the Habakkuk midrash, this leader was persecuted by a "wicked priest." There have been many attempts to identify these two personages with known historical figures of the second and first centuries B.C., but the newly published commentary on Nahum[2] makes one point at least very probable. The "wicked priest" must be King Alexander Jannaeus (104-78 B.C.), who on one occasion crucified eight hundred of his fellow-countrymen (Josephus *Ant.* xiii. 14. 2) — an incident referred to in the recently published Nahum midrash. But we still do not know the name of the Teacher of Righteousness, and there is no basis for the sensational theory that he was among those who were crucified.

This brings us to another question: did the Essenes regard their great teacher as the coming Messiah? If it could be proved that a past teacher was expected to return as Messiah — still more, if he had been crucified — it would be a startling anticipation of Christian faith in Jesus. Certainly the Damascus Document prophesies that "he who teaches righteousness" will arise at the end of the days. But does not this mean that he has already come, and that the Essenes are now living in the final age of the world's history? The Essenes also, as we have seen, expected a "Messiah from Aaron and Israel." André Dupont-Sommer, one of the first scholars to study the scrolls, goes so far as to think that, according to the belief of

---

[2] Conveniently accessible in T. H. Gaster, *The Dead Sea Scriptures* (Garden City, 1956), pp. 243-4.

the Qumran sect, the Teacher of Righteousness and the Messiah were one and the same. He bases part of his argument on a passage in the Habakkuk midrash, which in dealing with Hab. 2:4, "The just shall live by faith," says,

> Its interpretation concerns all who fulfil the Law in the house of Judah, whom God will rescue from the house of judgment because of their afflictions [or, their toil] and their faith in the Teacher of Righteousness.

His point is that the Teacher has become an object of faith. But the words of the Habakkuk midrash may mean no more than "faith" in him as an authoritative teacher, and the Hebrew may equally well be translated "by their fidelity to the Teacher of Righteousness."

There is, in fact, no evidence yet that the Qumran group regarded the lawgiver and the Messiah as identical. They are always mentioned separately, and usually in separate contexts. Indeed, in the Manual of Discipline the "Messiah of Israel" is subordinate to the priest. He is probably just Israel's anointed ruler.

The sect completely repudiated the Jerusalem priesthood and its sacrifices. The Pharisees had also protested against the crimes of the priestly leaders. But personal wickedness of the priests was not the sole reason for the hostility of the Qumran group. Those who controlled the Temple did not keep the high standard of ritual purity which the covenanters demanded, nor did they follow the Essene calendar, and therefore the worship itself was thought to be profaned. It is unlikely that the Dead Sea sect offered sacrifices in some place other than Jerusalem;

it is possible, as Josephus suggests in speaking of the Essenes, that they sent sacrifices or gifts to Jerusalem even if they did not participate personally. They taught, however, that when the laws of their Manual are observed in Israel it will be

> for divine favor of the land more than flesh of whole burnt offerings and than fats of sacrifice,
> while an offering of the lips is accounted as a fragrant offering of righteousness, and perfection of way as an acceptable freewill oblation (1QS 9:4-5).

Prayer and observance of the Law may have been their substitute for a sacrifice they could not conscientiously offer. This approaches the New Testament idea that the sacrifice pleasing to God consists of praise and sharing (Heb. 13:15-16). Certainly both praise and sharing were essential parts of the life of the order.

Thus the Dead Sea group was a completely organized community, with strong sociological and religious bonds. The various names given to it in the scrolls—"community" or "congregation" (*'edhah*), "unity" or "union" (*yahad*), "union of God" (*yahad 'El*), "covenant" (*berith*) or "covenant of God," "party" or "council" (*'esah*), "sons of light," "Chosen of God," "holy ones," and, of course, "Aaron and Israel"—suggest that it was strongly conscious of being the true Church of God. Because the Essenes withdrew from the world and made stringent demands on their converts, they have the sociological aspect of a sect, but in their own minds they were a universal Church with a world mission. The Christian Church used some of the same words to describe itself. Another term found in the Manual of Discipline, *ha-rabbim*, if it means "the many," i.e. the majority of the community, may be paralleled in the Book of Acts.

The parallels between the organization of the early Christian Church, as pictured in Acts, and that of the Essene community, are significant. The Qumran community was ruled by a group of twelve, or just possibly, fifteen men. The Manual of Discipline speaks of twelve men and three priests, and it is likely that the three are included in the twelve. Jerusalem Christianity at first was governed by the Twelve, with Peter originally at their head. In both cases the number twelve may correspond to the twelve tribes of Israel. The War Scroll speaks of twelve *sarîm* or princes of Israel who are leaders in the final age; their prototypes are the "princes" of Moses' time. The belief underlying the Christian practice undoubtedly is that the Twelve will be judges of the community in the coming Messianic age (Luke 22:29-30=Matt. 19:27-28). Later, of course, Peter leaves Jerusalem and the church in the city is led, according to Acts, by a council of "apostles and elders," with James the brother of the Lord acting as president in such a way that he is almost like a later monarchical bishop. We know of no single person in the Qumran community who corresponds exactly to James, and this is not surprising, since the brother of the Lord had a unique position. On the other hand, the Apostle Paul, when he tells of his own visit to Jerusalem, speaks of an inner group of three—James, Cephas (i.e. Peter), and John—who are regarded as "pillars" of the church there (Gal. 2:9). May it be that, as in the Essene group, there was a council which included an inner leadership of three men?

Both the Damascus Document and the Manual of Discipline mention an important official called the censor or inspector (*mebaqqer*). This is evidently the same person whom Josephus calls *epimeletes,* inspector or overseer, a word almost identical in meaning with *episkopos,* bishop. The *mebaqqer* presided at meetings, oversaw the administration of goods, and also examined and tried out candidates who wished to enter the community. In the Book of Acts, Peter and the apostles at first exercise such functions, which are afterward assigned to Stephen and the Seven (Acts 6:1-7). Now these are the duties which in later Christianity were committed to bishops and shared by them with the deacons, who were their assistants. Although the appointment of the Seven has traditionally been understood as the origin of the office of deacon, it is more likely that the story tells of the selection of the first bishops for the Greek-speaking wing of the Jerusalem church. After all, Stephen did not confine his work to administration; he preached and taught. One can only conjecture, but it may be that, as the Christian Church grew, the original small council could not care for all the community's needs, and there was a separation of functions similar to that which already existed among the Essenes. Perhaps by the end of the first century, certainly shortly after that, the Christian bishop was much more than the Essene *mebaqqer* —he was the chief liturgical officer as well as the superintendent—but there is a real parallel. Indeed one of the Qumran documents refers to the *mebaqqer* as a *paqid*— a term that corresponds closely to *episkopos* or bishop.

All this is striking enough, but the parallels between early Christianity and the Essenes go beyond outward organization and method. When we ask what the Qumran sect believed about man and sin and God's relation to man, we are immediately reminded of the deepest of the New Testament writers, St. Paul and the author of the Fourth Gospel.

Throughout the Gospel and First Epistle of John run the contrasts between light and darkness, truth and falsehood, which characterize the Qumran literature. The believers are sons of light, and, like their Lord, are from God. Their opponents are from the world, children of the devil. As in the Dead Sea scrolls, the two groups of men, bad and good, are not different in their essential natures. It is a moral difference; the children of light love the brethren and "do the truth," while the others hate light "because their deeds are evil." Furthermore, the present time is the decisive moment in history; it is the last hour, and the conflict between good and evil will soon come to its climax, indeed the drama is now being played out.

The Qumran literature sheds much light on the religious background of St. Paul's preaching and writing. The Hymns of Thanksgiving, and the hymn or rhapsody at the end of the Manual of Discipline, are the prayers of men who are deeply conscious of sin and the weakness—not to say depravity—of human nature. Man is only a thing of clay and water and without God there is no goodness or power in him. One is reminded of certain passages in the canonical Psalms but still more of the book known as IV Ezra (the II Esdras of the English Apocrypha) with its pessimistic view of humanity (see especially 7:116-126). But there is an equally strong belief that the sectarian worshipper has been instructed and made wise by God, forgiven, restored, and set on the right path. In the Manual of Discipline, God's righteousness or judgment (*mishpat*) is what vindicates, atones for, and cleanses the sinner. Here we have direct evidence that Paul was not the only man in

Judaism to discuss the problem of justification of the sinner. We know now what Hebrew words were the probable
equivalents of his Greek theological terms. If he ever had
occasion to discuss his faith in Hebrew or Aramaic he
would probably have used these, or related, words. Furthermore, although the Qumran authors were legalists, some
of them at least believed in salvation by grace. In the
Thanksgiving Psalms, the transformation of the personality is wrought by God's Holy Spirit. Faith in God's grace
was a part of the religious life of the Essenes, though we
have no evidence that they regarded faith itself as the
means of salvation. In fact, they believed in justification by
legal observance as well as faith.

Thus the Qumran sect and the early Church had certain features in common. They were communities of the
New Covenant; they were organized in similar ways; they
believed in the activity of the Holy Spirit in reclaiming
the sinner; they had sacred washings and common meals;
sometimes, at least, they had community property; they
taught love of the brethren; they appealed to a great
Teacher and looked for a Messiah and the establishment of
a new age; they had similar methods of interpreting scripture and used many of the same passages as proof texts;
and, while the Christians at times frequented the Temple,
both groups contained severe critics of the priesthood and
the cultus.

But here the similarities end. The chief difference, of
course, is that in the New Testament—and particularly
in John and Paul—Christ, his life, teaching and death, are
the essential fact of the New Covenant. Jesus is the authoritative teacher, but he is more. The new life is not merely
based on his teachings; it is a relationship to God through

him. His Person is central to the story, and faith is faith in him. The Teacher of Righteousness holds no such place in the hymns and prayers of the sect.

There are other important differences. The Qumran sect was, at least potentially, a military organization intending to fight a holy war. Christians may have believed that wars would precede the end of the age, but there is no sign that they expected to participate in them; quite the reverse. The Dead Sea group had an organization much more rigid and hierarchical than that of the Church. It distinguished three orders in the community, namely, priests, Levites and Israelites. Each had his permanent rank in the community and could neither rise nor fall. The lesser always had to obey the greater, and in the chapter meeting each man was asked for his counsel in strict order of rank. However, as Paul commanded the Corinthian church, so in the Qumran procedure each was to speak in turn and no one was to interrupt a speaker. The blessing was given by the priests, and only the sons of Aaron had jurisdiction in matters of law and property. The Damascus Document, in addition, sets up an elaborate system of judges who had to be not less than twenty-four nor more than sixty years old.

Early Christianity, of course, had no special privileges for members of the Jewish priesthood, though Acts tells us that a large number of priests joined the new religion (Acts 6:7). There were no special purity rules, no ritual of entering the Covenant, and no novitiate. At one time in Jerusalem communal ownership was practiced, though Acts takes care to say that the gift of Ananias and Sapphira was voluntary (5:4). In the churches founded by Paul there was some voluntary sharing, but no common store from which the community drew. Nor did these churches have a fixed organization—they were much less "Essene" in their aspect than the church in Jerusalem—in fact, Paul resisted all efforts of the Jerusalem church to extend its authority to them.

The author of the two-volume book Luke-Acts is in fact closer to the Qumran sect in his ideas than any other New Testament writer. He includes a large amount of material relating to John the Baptist and his disciples. John, whose ministry was carried on in the Jordan valley, was one of his great heroes. More than any evangelist Luke emphasizes the value of poverty. In his story of the Last Supper he quotes Jesus as saying, "This cup is the *new* covenant in my blood" (Luke 22:20). Here he agrees with Paul's account, while the parallel passages in Matthew and Mark do not use the word "new." Like Paul and like the hymn at the conclusion of the Manual of Discipline, he uses the verb "to justify," thereby showing some interest in the problem of how a sinner is justified in the sight of God. His gospel, like the Qumran literature and the Psalms of Solomon, includes hymns modelled on the canonical Psalms. Luke, as the Church's first historian, is interested in the beginnings of his religion and takes pains to picture its earliest phase from such fragmentary records as he has. Although he is also a follower of Paul, and although by the time he writes Christianity has begun to take a different form in the Gentile world, he is in close touch with the church in Jerusalem.

Jesus had given the Church no outward form; he had simply proclaimed the Kingdom of God. It was inevitable that when, after the Resurrection, the disciples gathered in Jerusalem, their community should take shape—perhaps unconsciously—from the only models its members knew, the Jewish brotherhoods and sects. We see certain resemblances to the baptist groups of the Dead Sea region. If we had more information about the Pharisaic *haburoth* we might find some of the the same characteristics in them also. In any case, the Jerusalem church was a natural development on Jewish soil.

· CHAPTER V ·

JESUS AND THE ESSENES

THE leaders of early Christianity were imaginative and creative; at the same time they were in close touch with the intellectual and religious life of Judaism. It therefore comes as no surprise that many features of the Qumran literature are paralleled in the Book of Acts, the letters of Paul, and the Gospel of John. Consciously or unconsciously, the first Christians expressed their message and organized their community in forms already present in Judaism. But are there significant contacts between the teaching of Jesus, as it is recorded in the synoptic gospels, and the sectarian documents?

The idea of perfection might seem to furnish such a contact. In Matt. 5:48, at the end of a section on the love of enemies, occurs the saying: "Therefore you shall be perfect as your heavenly Father is perfect." The parallel in Luke 6:36 instead of containing the word "perfect" reads "Be merciful, as your Father is merciful." Elsewhere in Matthew, when a rich man asks how he can attain eternal life, Jesus is quoted as saying, "If you wish to be perfect, go sell your property and give to the poor, and you will have treasure in heaven, and come follow me" (19:21). Here a contrast is made between the perfect and those who keep the commandments, but again the word "perfect" is absent from the parallels in Mark—which is Matthew's source—and Luke.

Perfection is an idea prominent in the Manual of Discipline. The believer must "walk before God perfectly" (1:8); the council of Twelve is composed of men who

are "perfect in all that is revealed of the whole Law"
(8:1-2); full members are called "men of perfection"
(8:20; 9:8); and God's counsel is "perfection of way"
(11:10-11; cf. 11:2). But in the Old Testament, as
Frederick Grant has shown, the Hebrew word which we
translate "perfect" never means ideal moral character or
sinless perfection such as Jews and Christians ascribe to
God. It describes a man who is integral, generally consistent in his behavior, sincere and right-dealing.[1] Paul
uses the corresponding Greek word *teleios* of the full-
grown or mature Christian. The same word in the Sermon
on the Mount (Matt. 5:48) must describe the man of
integrity, and one can imagine Jesus using it in this sense.
On the other hand, when it is employed in the Manual
of Discipline, it seems to refer to the special virtues of
the sect which by definition outsiders do not attain.
Matthew comes close to this meaning in his story of the
rich man. It almost appears that in 19:21 he has introduced the word to suggest that a really "perfect" Christian
can do heroic deeds not expected of other men.

Wisdom is another watchword of the Qumran literature. Late Jewish literature is full of the praise of wisdom.
The word is used first to denote those common-sense
maxims for successful living and morality that have been
handed down from previous generations. Toward the end
of the era before Christ it comes to include religious philosophy and the whole of God's gracious revelation, particularly his Law. It is almost equivalent to "education."
Rabbinic literature uses the term "the wise" to denote those
rabbis whose decisions have been approved.

Josephus, however, says that the Essenes had secret
books and a secret tradition of learning. This has been

[1] F. C. Grant, *The Earliest Gospel* (New York, 1943), pp. 218-23.

confirmed by the discovery in the Qumran caves of fragmentary books written in code. One wonders if the Manual
of Discipline was forbidden to outsiders. One who follows
its precepts must walk humbly "in the prudence of all
that is discreet according to the truth of the mysteries of
knowledge" (4:5-6). The latter part of the Manual contains some cryptic material, and it is said that God has
revealed his fountain of knowledge to the sect, and this
includes the "mystery to come" (11:3).

> My eye has beheld that wisdom
> Which was hidden from the men of knowledge,
> And that prudent purpose [which was hidden] from
>   the sons of men (11:6).

One is immediately reminded of the saying, "Blessed
are the eyes that see the things that you see; for I tell you
that many prophets and kings have wished to see what you
see and have not seen it, and to hear what you hear and
have not heard it" (Luke 10:23-24). In Luke this is
connected with the great saying about the special revelation given to the Son, and in Matt. 13:17 it is prefaced to
the interpretation of the parable of the Sower. A similar
rhapsody is found in I Cor. 2:9. This saying, which is
partly based on Isa. 64:3, was apparently known widely.

> What eye has not seen and ear has not heard,
> Nor has it entered into the heart of man—
> So many things that God has prepared for those who
>   love him.

Again there is a decided difference between the Dead
Sea sectaries and most other Jews. Wisdom for the Pharisees was not esoteric but open to any man willing to learn.
Although the rabbis had some secret speculations about the
wheels in Ezekiel, and reserved a few other teachings, these

were exceptions. The passage from First Corinthians quoted above is in a section devoted to the mystery of the Gospel. Paul says, it is true, that he utters wisdom among the perfect; and it is a wisdom that was not known to the rulers of the world, otherwise they would not have crucified the Lord of glory (2:1-8). But in subsequent paragraphs, he contrasts this wisdom of God, which is foolishness to men, with some subtle philosophy ("wisdom of men") which the Corinthians have been only too willing to accept. It appears that the divine wisdom is no longer hidden from men; if it makes foolishness to them and they do not accept it, it is only because they are unwilling to be humble.

The saying of Jesus quoted by Matthew and Luke is apparently a floating word which each of the evangelists has put into a context which he deems appropriate. Luke attaches it to the self-revelation of Jesus—a passage unique in the synoptic gospels—and Matthew to the parable of the Sower. Matthew is simply developing further one of Mark's ideas. Mark, like Paul and other early Christians, baffled by the unwillingness of the Jewish people to accept the Gospel, assumed that Jesus' teaching must have been misunderstood—still more, God must have veiled it from all but the elect. Both Mark and Matthew therefore picture Jesus as adding private interpretations to the parables of the Kingdom—explanations which, as in the case of the parable of the Sower, do not always fit the original meaning of the parable.

Most New Testament scholars now agree that the interpretations of the parables are examples of early Christian preaching, and that the parables—far from being veiled, esoteric teaching—were illustrations designed to make Jesus' meaning luminous to anyone willing to listen. If sometimes they are obscure to the modern reader, it is usually because we do not know the original context in which they were spoken. What, then, is the meaning of "Blessed are the eyes that see the things that you see"? The saying probably referred originally to the Good News proclaimed by Jesus and to the wonderful events that accompanied it—healing, casting out of demons, and the repentance and new life of the poor and humble. The message was not totally new—there is Good News in the Old Testament—but now dramatically God, through Jesus, is making that message effective in the world.

Matthew, like Paul, is not uninfluenced by the sectarian idea of wisdom spoken to the perfect. Though Jesus' teaching had been public and the early Christians did not conceal their doctrines, Paul and the Evangelists believed that perhaps God had temporarily blinded the minds of unbelievers.

Another area of contact may be religious law. We have direct evidence from the letters of Paul that Christians had to face the problem of regulation of life in the community, settlement of disputes, and decision of difficult moral questions. Paul laid down before the Corinthians the Old Testament rule of evidence: "at the mouth of two or three witnesses every word shall be established" (II Cor. 13:1). The Church also had to have the prerogative of excommunicating serious sinners, though the ban should not be permanent and penitents should be welcomed back (I Cor. 5:13; II Cor. 2:6-11). Nor is this excommunication merely exclusion from a voluntary society; Paul says that he has decided on the action, just as if he were present with the Corinthians; that when the church of Corinth meets, presumably as a worshipping congregation, his own spirit and the power of the Lord Jesus will be present also; and the Corinthians must hand the offender over to Satan for the destruction of the flesh so that his spirit may be saved in the day of the Lord (I Cor. 5:3-5).

Similar ideas are to be found in sayings ascribed to Jesus in the eighteenth chapter of Matthew. A believer with a grievance against his brother should first try to win him to repentance by reproving him. If the offender proves recalcitrant, the plaintiff is to take two or three witnesses and remonstrate with him again; and if this is unavailing, the matter may then be reported to the church. If, finally, the offender defies the church's judgment, "let him be to you as the heathen and the tax collector" (Matt. 18:17). Linked with this last are three other sayings: (1) Whatever the church binds or looses on earth will be bound or loosed in heaven; (2) Where two or three agree in a request it will be granted "by my Father who is in heaven"; (3) "Where two or three are gathered together in my name, there am I in the midst of them" (18:18-20). The first of these sayings must originally have referred to the rabbinic power of binding and loosing, i.e. declaring something forbidden or permitted, and the other two properly refer to prayer. When brought into this artificial context, the total effect is the same as Paul's teaching on excommunication; and it is significant that the chapter concludes with the parable of the Unforgiving Slave. The church must give mercy to the penitent for an unlimited number of times. Just so, Paul bade the Corinthians welcome back the man who had been excluded.

The Manual of Discipline and the Damascus Document contain some remarkable parallels to these teachings of Matthew and Paul. There are several rules for reproof and accusation in the Damascus Document. The Manual does not go into as great detail, but it apparently provides that an accuser must reprove his fellow in the presence of witnesses before he can bring an accusation in the presence of the Many (1QS 6:1); according to the majority a divinely guided decision is reached (5:3).

Matthew dealt with the problem of hard cases at law by including traditions that the power to bind and loose had first been given to Peter and then to the church (16:19; 18:18). Peter is therefore pictured as the ideal rabbi, whose decisions can be relied on, but the church meeting as a whole is also an authoritative court. One example of binding and loosing in the Gospel of Matthew itself would seem to be the famous exception clause in the saying which prohibits divorce ("Whoever divorces his wife *except for the cause of fornication* causes her to commit adultery," 5:32; cf. 19:9). This exception clause is not found in Mark and Luke and many scholars now regard it as an addition to the original saying. The church for which Matthew writes has already relaxed the law in the case where the man's wife has been found guilty of unchastity, and Matthew goes so far as to attribute the church's rule to Jesus himself. Paul had similarly to decide when divorce might be tolerated, but did so on his own responsibility (I Cor. 7:12-16). The two approaches illustrate the difference between Matthew and Paul: the former works within the framework of rabbinic law, the latter regards even the words of Jesus as directives which the individual—or the apostle—must interpret in the light of conscience.

It is with some frankness that the Manual of Discipline and the Damascus Document face the problem of new Law. Not only did the sect have the Old Testament, its founder, and its own sacred books; it believed that the community itself had the power and right to enact laws which were binding until the coming of the future age when God should visit the earth (1QS 8:9; Damascus Document [henceforth cited as CDC] 13:20–14:2).

Another provision of the sectarian writings is paralleled in Matthew and the Epistle of James but not elsewhere. This is the rejection of oaths. The Damascus Document forbade oaths by the commonly used names of God—El, Elohim, and Adonai. Of course the most sacred name Yahweh could not even be pronounced. Yet some kind of oath or vow had to be taken by those who joined the order. This involved a promise to return to the Law of Moses with all one's heart and soul, and it invoked "the curses of the covenant" on those who failed to keep the promise" (CDC 15:5-10). A woman's oath was annulled if the keeping of it led to transgression of the covenant. Vows must have been permitted, for certain of them are held not to be binding.

Jesus taught his disciples not to take oaths at all (Matt. 5:33-37), for anything more than Yes or No is from the evil one. The implication is that use of God's name in an oath dishonors him. To swear by anything else is to swear by that which God has created and which is in his power, not man's. This teaching is echoed in simpler form in Jas. 5:12, and Matt. 23:16-22 ridicules rabbinic distinctions between valid and invalid oaths.

There are three possible reasons for Jesus' decision. (1) Simple truthfulness is sufficient and should characterize the religious man. The setting up of oaths and rules for them implies that one need not always tell the truth but sometimes can be compelled to do so out of fear of God. (2) The religious oath implies that God is called upon to punish untruth. But this invades God's sovereign power and tries to put him under compulsion from man to punish in a given instance. (3) Rules about valid and invalid oaths bring the whole matter into discredit and degrade all oaths into the kind of idle swearing which is all too common; the only remedy for profanity is to sweep away oaths and rely on a simple affirmation. Any of these three interpretations would be in harmony with Jesus' general outlook. We do not know what motive lay behind the Essene rejection of oaths. Since members of the sect were rigorists in their approach to moral problems, perhaps the third of these considerations moved them.

How far do these sayings in Matthew—on oaths and church discipline—represent the authentic teaching of Jesus?

The prohibition of oaths furnishes no particular problem. Because Matthew and the church of his neighborhood were interested in matters of Jewish law, they may have passed on a tradition of this sort while other Christians forgot it. The question whether Jesus left a kind of legal constitution for the Church, with provision for interpretation of law and settlement of disputes, is more difficult and serious.

For three reasons it is unlikely that he gave such legislation. In the first place, Matthew is the only evangelist who is particularly interested in law and organization. Mark and Luke find the center of Christianity elsewhere than in church order. This is not because they are followers of Paul; it is because of the gospel tradition itself. Matthew's gospel is the only one to use the word *ekklesia*, which we translate "church." Matthew presents the Sermon on the Mount as a new Law, and thinks of the command of the risen Christ in rabbinical terms: Jesus' followers are to make disciples of all nations, baptize them, and teach them all that he has commanded. None of the other gospels contains sayings of this sort. Even John, who has a high sense of the religious meaning of the Church and its power to exclude or forgive, does not define it in legal terms. Luke pictures a regular church organization in Jerusalem, and councils of presbyters in churches outside Palestine, but traces back to Jesus no more than the appointment of the original Twelve.

Second, the sayings which Matthew uses in his section on church organization are taken out of context, and he uses them in a sense not originally intended. He has employed them atomistically, just as he and the Dead Sea writers use passages from the Old Testament. Since he feels so strongly that a thing *must* be so, then it must be in the sacred words of the Old Testament or of Jesus, if only they can be given the right interpretation.

Finally, there is a serious question about some of the sayings themselves. It is hard to imagine Jesus saying that a recalcitrant must be treated as a heathen and a tax-collector (Matt. 18:17), for he went to such people with the Good News and forgiveness. It is the Pharisees, not Jesus, who usually reject the heathen and the tax-collectors. I also doubt that Jesus conveyed to Peter a sweeping "power of the keys" or the right to bind and loose. The whole passage (Matt. 16:17-19) is absent from Mark, which Matthew used, and from Luke. It looks like the attempt of an enthusiastic follower, to whom Peter was a hero and saint, to avoid the difficulties raised by the Gospel of Mark. Mark tells us that at Caesarea Philippi, when Peter hailed Jesus as the Messiah, Jesus bade him be silent and later rebuked him, calling him Satan (Mark 8:29-33). How could it be wrong to express the fundamental faith of the Jewish Christians? Surely something must be lacking in Mark. Therefore some follower of Peter, perhaps from an ecstatic revelation, added the words of praise: "Blessed are you, Simon, son of Jonah, for flesh and blood has not revealed it to you, but my Father who is in the heavens" (Matt. 16:17). To this were added other traditions dear to the Petrine wing of the church, committing to Peter the power to make legal decisions. The words "my Father who is in the heavens" are a familiar mark of Matthew's style, and the phrase "flesh and blood" recalls Paul's statement that when God revealed his Son to him he had not conferred with flesh and blood. The answer of Peter's followers was that his revelation, too, was not mediated in any way by flesh and blood.

It appears, then, that Matthew's interest in the Church as guarantor of a new legal tradition is to be ascribed to the evangelist and not to Jesus. This apparent point of contact with the Qumran literature is therefore not significant so far as Jesus himself is concerned.

But even though this is so, there may be places where specific rulings of the Qumran sect may be compared with specific sayings of Jesus on matters of law. The teaching about oaths, found only in Matthew and James, was one example. Elsewhere in the synoptic gospels there are other instances.

The Qumran sectary was required to keep the Sabbath day, the fast day (presumably the Day of Atonement) and other appointed days, according to strict and exact rules. No one was allowed to help an animal that gave birth on the Sabbath. If the newborn animal fell into a cistern or pit it was not lawful to pull it out even to save its life, though one might rescue a human being from such a place. Food lying in the field could not be collected and eaten on the Sabbath. This last is similar to the Pharisaic ruling which forbade eating fruit which had fallen from trees on the Sabbath.

Here certainly is one place where Jesus taught something radically different. Mark contains two Sabbath controversies. In one of them, the plucking of grain (Mark 2:23-28), Jesus' disciples are presumably accused of reaping and threshing—two of the thirty-nine classes of work which the Pharisees prohibited on the Sabbath. His defense is not that the amount was trifling but that the disciples, like David and his men, were hungry. In the controversy over healing (3:1-6) he asks a question that his opponents would have considered beside the point: "Is it lawful to do good on the Sabbath or to do evil, to save a life or to kill?" From the point of view of the Pharisees—and probably the Essenes too—the obligation to save life overrode the Sabbath. But Jesus' saying implies that to neglect doing a deed of mercy, merely because it is the Sabbath, is to do evil. Human need is in both cases the criterion.

Luke has two additional cases of Sabbath healing. In one of them Jesus heals a woman with a badly stooped back (Luke 13:10-16), and his answer to the criticism is that on the Sabbath one will loose an ox or an ass to water him, therefore it is right to loose this woman who has been bound by Satan for eighteen years. The case of the dropsical man (14:2-6) contains the argument that if a man's ox or son (some manuscripts have "ass" in place of "son") falls into the pit he will pull him out. Matthew inserts this argument into his form of the story of the man with withered hand (Matt. 12:9-14). In the first century there was apparently no agreement about aid to an animal on the Sabbath—Galileans no doubt took the "liberal" position —but in any event Jesus' position is clear: human need is so important that one ought not to wait till the end of the Sabbath to alleviate misery and bring happiness.

Another controversy has to do with the Corban vow. This might conceivably teach us something about Jesus' relation to the Qumran sect as well as to the Pharisees. In Mark 7:11-13 Jesus accuses the Pharisees of departing from the commandment of God to follow their own tradition, because they say that if a man makes a vow by the gift (*qurban*) in the Temple not to benefit his father or mother—or perhaps if he vows to the Temple what he would have given them—he must keep the vow. Possibly the Qumran sect would have agreed with Jesus; the Damascus Document did not permit a man to declare holy to God "the food of his mouth" (16:14). We know, too, that by the end of the first century A.D., at any rate, the Pharisees ruled as Jesus did: if a vow involved detriment to father or mother it could be revoked. It may be that at the time of Jesus' ministry some groups of Pharisees took the rigorist position; or it may have been some other party. The motive of Jesus was not only human need but obedience to a fundamental commandment, and he probably approved of vows as little as of oaths.

Jesus' teaching on divorce has been compared with that of the Damascus Document. As against the school of Hillel, which permitted divorce for any cause, he took a position similar to that of the school of Shammai, but more strict (Mark 10:2-9; we have already argued that the exception clause of Matt. 5:32; 19:9 cannot go back to Jesus). His reason is that, while Moses permitted divorce because of the hardness of man's heart, the fundamental purpose of God as shown in Genesis is lifelong marriage: "Male and female he created them; for this cause a man shall leave his father and mother, and the two shall be one flesh. What therefore God has joined, let not man separate."

The parallel passage from the Damascus Document is worth quoting, obscure though it is:

> The builders of the wall, who have walked after *saw*
> —the *saw* is a preacher, because it says, "They will
> surely preach"—they are caught in two nets in forni-
> cation: by taking two women in their lifetime, though
> the principle of the creation is, "Male and female he
> created them," and those who went into the ark,
> "Two by two they went into the ark" (CDC 7:1-3).

The "builders of the wall" are a mysterious feature of the Damascus Document. Obviously, they are false teachers, and they daub with whitewash the wall they have built. The reference is apparently to Ezek. 13:10. Because the Pharisees built a fence about the Law, and because Jesus is quoted as saying that they are "whited sepulchres," one is tempted at first to identify the builders of the wall with the Pharisees. But some of the practices of these builders which are denounced in the Damascus Document were also rejected by the Pharisees. There is also a real question whether the passage in the Damascus Document applies to divorce, since it could more naturally refer to polygamy. But it is significant that in a matter involving marriage both Jesus and the sectarian writer use the Genesis passage to teach monogamy. Jesus' motive, however, is not the desire to establish a perfect theocracy in which the older and stricter traditions can be kept. It is the attempt to get behind the specific provision of the Law to its spirit and heart.

Matthew also contains, and in the context of the divorce discussion, a saying that "there are those who have made themselves eunuchs for the sake of the Kingdom of the heavens" (Matt. 19:12). The disciples have just observed that if the only permissible cause for divorce is unchastity, perhaps it is better not to marry. Certainly this attitude, which is ascribed to the disciples, reminds one of Josephus' remark that the Essenes believed no woman could be faithful to one man. In both cases women are distrusted, and once again there is an apparent contact between Matthew's special material and the Essenes. We must, however, remember that the Dead Sea literature thus far discovered says nothing about celibacy.

The saying ascribed to Jesus should be considered apart from its somewhat artificial context. There is no suggestion in it that celibacy is demanded of more than the few who are specially called to it. Jeremiah was told that he should not marry because most children to be born in the near future would be slain in the coming war (Jer. 16:2-4). Paul likewise counselled celibacy because, in view of the shortness of this present age, he thought it better for a man to be without cares and worries (I Cor. 7:25-35). There are records of several rabbis who remained unmarried because they were so occupied with Torah that they wished to be free from family responsibilities. The brief saying of Jesus, however, is not based on any of these concerns. It is only another way of saying that the Kingdom of God takes precedence of all other claims on one's life (cf. Mark 10:28-30; Luke 9: 57-62).

Jesus and the Qumran sect are radically different in their attitude to enemies. Claude Montefiore and other liberal Jewish scholars have objected to Jesus' formulation, "You have heard that it was said, 'You shall love your neighbor and hate your enemy'" (Matt. 5:43) on the ground that it was an unfair summary; Judaism never taught such a thing.[2] But the Dead Sea law, at any rate, did teach its observers to hate their enemies. They were to keep strictly away from "unclean" outsiders, not to work with them, share their food or drink, or accept anything from them except for a price (1QS 2:19–3:6; 5:1, 14-17). The Damascus Document provided that all trade with "children of the Pit" had to be for cash, and agreements with them must be approved by the overseer of the camp (CDC 13: 14-16).

Now of course it is true that one passage in the Manual bids the sectarian "to respond humbly before the haughty of spirit, and with broken spirit to the men of injustice" (1QS 11:1-2). Yet in other places he is commanded to love all the sons of light but hate the sons of darkness (1:9-10), and to keep an eternal secret hatred toward the men of the Pit "while one abandons to them property and labor of hands as a slave [does] to him who rules and shows humility before him who lords it over him" (9:21-23). The sectarian, to be sure, says, "I will repay no man with evil's due; with good will I pursue a man," but this is because vengeance belongs to God alone (10:18). He must not keep his anger against those who repent, but he feels no responsibility to console or help them so long as they are wicked (10:20-21).

The gospels now and then tell of Jesus manifesting anger and indignation—particularly against hypocrisy and the cruelty of religious people. This need not conflict with his teaching against hatred of enemies. Surely one who loves his enemies can make a moral judgment, and express it with vivid emotion. Jesus commands his disciples to love their enemies not because this is prudent, or even

[2] C. G. Montefiore, *The Synoptic Gospels,* 2nd ed. (London, 1927), II, pp. 77-80.

out of hope of the enemy's conversion, but simply because
one must imitate the outgoing lovingkindness of God, who
returns good for evil (Matt. 5:43-48). This teaching is
reinforced by the preceding section, which bids men turn
the other cheek and go a second mile when compelled
to go one (5:38-42). The Qumran sectary's outward
behavior may be similar to that which Jesus commands,
but the inner spirit is different. In Jesus' words there is no
overtone of secret hatred or resentment, or prayer that
God will maintain the believer's cause and give vengeance
—Paul has remnants of this earlier attitude in Rom. 12:19-
21—but so far as Jesus is concerned, love of enemies must
be genuine.[3] Elsewhere in Jewish teaching nothing like
this is found. The rabbis go no further than to teach that
a man must not rejoice over the misfortune of his enemy,
and must not recompense evil with evil.

In still other respects there are great differences between Jesus and the Dead Sea covenanters. Jesus is quite
unconcerned with the issues of priesthood and sacrifice.
For the most part he appears to take for granted this
aspect of Judaism. The leper is told to go and show himself to the priests so that he may be restored to his place
in the community (Mark 1:44); he could not have carried
on a normal life without official priestly inspection and a
sacrifice. The offering of gifts at the altar was a continual
occurrence and Jesus does not concern himself with the
merits of this religious custom; what is important to him
is that a man must first be reconciled with his brother,
otherwise he cannot presume to come into the presence of
God (Matt. 5:23-24). In the light of this saying, we may
suppose that Jesus' cleansing of the Temple was neither

---

[3] In the Gospel of John and First Epistle of John, however, the emphasis
is entirely on love within the Christian community.

a protest against sacrifice as such nor a demand that the sacrificial system be brought to perfection; his attitude is neither that of Stephen, who regarded the building of the Temple as a sin (Acts 7:46-50), nor of the Manual of Discipline. It was, instead, a warning that current practice was destroying the very purpose for which the Temple was founded. What he had previously said about prayer, fasting and almsgiving was now dramatically applied to the Temple. We are left with the impression that for Jesus all these religious practices are means to an end. The difference is that the sectarians regarded the keeping of sacrificial laws as ends in themselves; God had commanded that sacrifice be carried on and in a specific and fixed way.

It is not surprising, therefore, that in Jesus' teaching there is no special place for priests and Levites. Nor is there any clear evidence that he provided a hierarchy to take their place. In the earliest sources—Mark, Q, and the special material of Luke—no legal authority is ascribed to the twelve most intimate disciples of Jesus. They are sent to help in Jesus' work of announcing the Kingdom, and the stories about them show that the evangelists thought of the Twelve as examples to other believers—examples of mature and immature faith, unbelief, weakness, perplexity and heroism. Only at a later stage is the office of apostle or travelling missionary traced back to the Twelve. Even in the eighteenth chapter of Matthew, which reflects to so great a degree the growing self-consciousness of the Church, and its need for legal arrangements, the authority is not confined to Peter or the Twelve but reposes in the congregation.

There seems to have been no formal ritual or ceremony for entering the group of Jesus' disciples. Jesus may have accepted John's rite of baptism but the evidence is not certain, and the formal establishment of Christian baptism comes only after the resurrection. There do seem to have been sacred meals. The Last Supper was one, the Feeding of the Five Thousand was another. At the Last Supper, Jesus promised that he would drink wine with the disciples again in the Kingdom of God (Mark 14:25). The Feeding is reminiscent of the miracle of the manna, and John 6:49-51 makes this reference explicit. For early Christians these solemn gatherings were an anticipation of the Messianic Banquet, when, as in the days of Moses, all God's people would be fed.

There is no record that Jesus urged formal study or meditation. The earliest followers were not rabbinical disciples, whose master taught them a tradition over several months or years, but men who were entrusted with a simple message to broadcast. We hear of Jesus reading the lesson in the synagogue, but there is no record of his having engaged in formal studies. He was, of course, well acquainted with the Hebrew Bible and must have had some instruction in the local synagogue.

Perhaps partly because he was not trained in the rabbinical schools, Jesus did not indulge in the elaborate scriptural interpretation which marks both the Dead Sea sect and many early Christian writers. Of the evangelists, Matthew is the one most given to ingenious use of Old Testament quotations. An example is his use of Isa. 53:4, "he took our sicknesses and bore our diseases," to apply to Jesus' healing activity (Matt. 8:17). The psychology of the evangelist, like that of the authors of Acts and First Peter, is similar to that of the Dead Sea writers: events of recent religious history are thought to have been prefigured, sometimes explicitly prophesied, by the authors of the Old Testament. The evangelists do not usually ascribe these interpretations to Jesus himself.

On the few occasions when the synoptic gospels represent him as quoting the Old Testament, Jesus' use is ordinarily straightforward. He tells the story of David eating the loaves of presentation (Mark 2:25-26), and this is a straight historical example. When he quotes Isaiah's complaint that the people honor God with their lips but their heart is far from him (Mark 7:6-7), he makes a contemporary application but in the spirit of the original prophecy. In the divorce controversy he appeals beyond the Mosaic permission of divorce to the intention of God as originally disclosed. This perhaps involves reading something into the original text but it shows that Jesus' intent was to arrive at God's fundamental purpose. It is basically a dependence on the message of scripture itself. Even the quotation of biblical texts in the Temptation story (Matt. 4:4, 7, 10=Luke 4:4, 8, 12) is simple and natural. Jesus' way was to turn to the fundamental and clearly expressed ideas of the Old Testament. On one occasion he applies an ancient prophecy to present events when he says, "The blind see again and the lame walk, lepers are cleansed and the deaf hear, the dead are raised and the poor receive good news" (Matt. 11:5=Luke 7:22). This typological approach is found everywhere in the New Testament and late Judaism: God's gracious deeds of the past find their counterpart in the present and the future. It is, however, more of an allusion and an example than a claim that recent happenings are a formal fulfillment of prophecy. Jesus' message does not stand or fall with such fulfillments. So far as he is concerned, truth authenticates itself.

CHAPTER VI

THE AREA OF CONFLICT

JESUS, then, did not emerge from one of the parties or sects. At one time he was so closely associated with John the Baptist that he accepted baptism. The disciples of the Baptist constitute the only group that he can be said to have joined, and he did not remain a part of it. After John's arrest—perhaps even before it—he carried on an independent ministry with a message of his own. There is no reason to think that in his lifetime John founded a sect, though after his death his movement may have become one. John was a hermit, a prophetic voice, a baptizer, who called upon Israel to repent before it should be too late. Both he and Jesus must have come out of the mass of undifferentiated Jews, who belonged to no party, but believed in God and the Old Testament, attended the synagogues, kept the traditions as their fathers had done, and hoped for the time when God would restore Israel to independence and bring peace and righteousness. They were far from the sophistication of the city scholars and had scant interest in their controversies; on the other hand, they were unlike their heedless neighbors who wanted neither legal discussions nor religion. The Bible was their principal source of knowledge and inspiration and they read it for themselves. There must have been many such people in synagogues where no rabbi or expert was at hand, though there were never enough of them to awaken the people to their responsibilities.

Through everything that Jesus said about oaths, divorce, and the Sabbath law, runs the conviction that man is a free but responsible moral agent. This does not mean that he is perfect; it does not rule out the possibility that in man's freedom he might choose sin or the fact that his freedom is seriously hampered by his sin. Jesus knew that men were sinners and did not minimize the fact; on the other hand, he did not concentrate on the weakness of man's will—he was more interested in God's strengthening love —and he seems to have believed that freedom should be exercised. He differed from the Pharisees in believing that the average person, and not merely the expert, has the responsibility to make moral decisions and act on them. He was once quoted as saying, "Why do you not judge for yourselves what is right?" (Luke 12:57)—a stray remark that we might be inclined to discount if it did not fit so well with his attitude to the Law as seen elsewhere. Man, it would appear from Jesus' actions and rulings, has the right and duty to decide which matters of the Law are most important; and if some of the minutiae of the Law as then understood tended to deflect man from his most important duties, then these lesser matters could safely be disregarded and set aside.

Lest there be any misunderstanding, let it be said once again that this is not the attitude of the "ordinary layman" or Galilean peasant who is impatient of what the preachers say. It is the attitude of one who has God and God's business constantly in his mind. But it is surely a very independent line, as sympathetic Jewish scholars are not slow to point out. They are sometimes baffled by the un-Jewishness of the teachings about oaths and divorce. How can it be called a "fulfillment of the Law" to forbid these? It is at the very least an extreme case of private judgment, for it means setting aside not the oral but the written Law.

The only way to account for Jesus' approach is to say

that he put God first and the biblical Law second, even though to the Pharisees this seemed an unreal distinction. But this had been the approach of the prophets; otherwise, they would have said "the tradition says" and not "thus saith the Lord." For although the Bible was then, as it is now, the supreme source of the knowledge of God, it points beyond itself to him. Jesus was able to discern the character of God in the Bible, and from that point on he knew which words of the Hebrew Law and Prophets were truest to that character.

Anything that we say about his motives has to be in the nature of careful and reverent guesswork, a reading between the lines, based on the best historical examination of the sources we can manage. There have been many well-meaning attempts to speculate on the "Messianic self-consciousness of Jesus" or his "filial consciousness" but they are mostly failures. Jesus did not speak about his inner life or describe how he came to his conclusions; nor do the evangelists, with the exception of John, picture him as doing so. He spoke about God and God's will with complete sureness and seems to have taken it for granted that candid and receptive people would recognize the truth of his words.

It has even been pointed out that Jesus gives no indication of being in constant conscious communion with God. As Henry Cadbury says, a number of his parables and sayings picture God in the figure of an *absent* master; the good slave is the one who goes on working when he has neither the fear nor the encouragement of his Lord's presence.[1] This is no doubt a real and constant relation-

[1] H. J. Cadbury, *Jesus: What Manner of Man* (New York, 1947), pp. 42-48.

ship with God, but Jesus' emphasis is certainly not on his emotionally or mystically felt presence, but on the reality and constant availability of God, his never-ceasing fatherly care, and his unfailing forgiveness and judgment. Though God is pictured as king, landlord and master, he is above all Father. Here Jesus is not unique—the Jewish liturgy addresses God as "Our Father who art in heaven" and it is no mere formality—but the difference is that to Jesus the fatherhood of God has immediate, practical consequences—in interpreting the biblical Law as in other ways. Jesus knows God as Father and relies on him completely; therefore he knows what the Father wishes, and with complete inner certainty.

A second, and closely related, conviction of Jesus was that he and his followers had been enlisted to proclaim God's Kingdom and to bring its blessings to those who needed them most. He emphasized God's gracious promise rather than the duties involved in discipleship. The duties were real and serious enough; all through the gospel the warnings and the promises run side by side; but what was needed was the news that God had acted first, he had taken the first step in man's direction. He had forgiven and blessed, without reservations; thereupon it was man's business to believe, repent and do.

One dramatic instance of this teaching is the story of the paralytic let down through the roof (Mark 2:1-12). Instead of speaking a word of healing, Jesus says, "Child, your sins are forgiven." The criticism of the Pharisees is not difficult to understand. They believed that God unfailingly forgave sins *if the sinner was genuinely repentant*. But how could Jesus know that the man was repentant and so pronounce the forgiveness? Only God could know such a thing.

The evangelist, being a Christian, did not have the same view of the situation. To him the words "but that you may know that the Son of Man has power on earth to forgive sins" (2:10) meant that the heavenly Son of Man, the future judge, now temporarily on earth, possessed the full prerogatives of God. But was this the reason for Jesus' action? "Son of Man" was a familiar Semitic way of saying "a human being"; and if Jesus spoke this word he may have meant, "Man has now the power to pronounce the forgiveness on behalf of God." At least Matthew, in the parallel passage, says, "the crowds, when they saw it, feared and glorified God, who had given such power to men" (Matt. 9:8).

Jesus, then, came with the message of God's antecedent forgiveness, and it was the duty and privilege of man to proclaim the good news of this. Whatever one thinks of the story of the paralytic, the gospel involved the free offer of God's love and help. God is the shepherd looking for the lost sheep, the father of the Prodigal Son who waits for no word of repentance, the owner of the vineyard who hires laborers without bargaining and is more generous than they expect. When Jesus sent his followers to preach the coming of the Kingdom, the message undoubtedly included this word of forgiveness.

This attitude toward sinners came into conflict with an important part of the Pharisaic program: separation from sin and sinners. We must realize that the Pharisaic brother-hoods gladly accepted the repentant sinner.[2] But while he remained in his sin he must be avoided. Pharisaism seems

[2] Montefiore, *Synoptic Gospels*, I, p. 55.

to have begun as a voluntary association of men who tried to keep the Law, to eat pure foods, and to remain pure by avoiding defiling contacts. The Essene movement was a more extreme example of the same impulse.

Jesus, in contrast to this, remarks that "the healthy do not need a physician but those who are sick" (Mark 2:17). This expresses concisely the fundamental difference between his attitude and that of the Pharisees. Instead of forming a separatist party, with strict requirements of membership, he seeks out sinners and does not fear contact with them.

The scandalized protest of Jesus' opponents shows that this was something new in the Judaism of the first century. "See—a glutton and a winesoak, a friend of tax-collectors and sinners" (Luke 7:34=Matt. 11:19). Jesus' answer to the taunt is that nothing can satisfy these critics, for John the Baptist was accustomed to fast from food and drink and he was regarded as insane. The saying illustrates not only our Lord's method in dealing with the sinner but the tone of joy in which he carried on his mission. Withdrawal and fasting are left behind as inappropriate.

The saying links up, too, with one of his most important parables, that of the Great Supper (Luke 14:16-24=Matt. 22:1-10). Jesus has a vocation to seek out sinners, but it is more than that. He takes this attitude because it is the attitude of God himself, summoning into his Kingdom the poor, the maimed, the halt and the blind (Luke 14:21)— and this is a moment of great rejoicing, symbolized by the famous picture of the Messianic Banquet. There is a reason why the message comes particularly to the outcasts. It could be spoken to all men, but at some stage of his ministry Jesus has concluded that the natural heirs of the Kingdom

—the most earnest and serious religious leaders of the nation—have rejected it, and their place must be taken by others.

No teaching of Jesus is more richly attested than this. The elder brother begrudges the welcome given the Prodigal Son; the men who were hired early in the morning to work in the vineyard complain that late comers have received the same wage as those who have borne the burden of the day and the scorching heat. Explanations did no good: "Child, you are always with me, and everything that I have is yours" (Luke 15:31) or "Is it not lawful for me to do what I will on my own domain? Are you going to be grudging because I am generous?" (Matt. 20:15). On the one hand, the critics felt no need of further repentance —they themselves had done what was required ("Never at any time have I transgressed your commandment," Luke 15:29)—on the other hand, they could not see why the religious possession they had worked so hard to achieve should be freely and unconditionally offered to others.

From the point of view of both Pharisees and Essenes the message of Jesus was even worse than this. It broke down moral standards; it obliterated the distinction between the serious-minded and the heedless, godless multitudes; at best it sounded like sentimentality and emotionalism, at worst it called in question Jesus' own moral fibre. One can easily imagine what some of the critics said: "He who touches pitch shall be defiled"; "a man is known by the company he keeps."

When Jesus and the Pharisees came finally into collision over the purity laws, another basic issue was disclosed. This is a more serious point of difference than most of the others, for it is not merely concerned with religious strategy;

it affects the authority of the written Law and the fundamental bond which was thought to hold the Jewish community together—the concept of a holy people separated
from Gentile defilement. The rules for purity in Leviticus
are only one part of the Pentateuch, but they are a very
prominent part. I can remember how, as a child, I read
large sections of the Bible, beginning with Genesis, and
puzzled over the many commandments that were not kept
by us or any of our neighbors, though this was presumably
our Bible! The levitical prescriptions had a tremendous
social power in maintaining the separateness of Judaism,
as many conservative Jews in modern Israel and elsewhere
understand quite well. The Pharisees heightened the separateness of Judaism—not for conscious purposes of social
control as though they were modern propagandists, but
out of zeal for God and his Law. They seem to have applied the old priestly rules of purity to laymen on the
principle that it is good for all God's people to manifest
the same holiness as priests. Mark 7:3-4 gives a vivid
contemporary picture of them sprinkling themselves when
they return from the *agora*, washing hands before they
eat, and purifying vessels; all this, it is said, is part of the
"tradition of the elders."

In a saying which comes down to us from the Q source,
Jesus accuses the Pharisees of cleansing the outside of the
cup while the inside remains filthy (Matt. 23:25-26=Luke
11:39-41). This is metaphorical, because the Mishnah is
concerned for the ritual cleanliness of the inside of vessels.
Jesus here draws the distinction between ritual purity of
body and evil dispositions within. The saying of Mark
7:15 is even more radical, for it states flatly that *nothing*
which enters into a man from outside can defile him; and
this is only a step beyond the Q saying, for both seem to

teach that only inner purity is important, and this cannot be attained by external means.

Such a statement would have been profoundly disturbing to the Pharisees. It is not just "the tradition of the elders" that is attacked, not the new elaboration of purity rules, but the institution of purity itself. This is more dangerous than Jesus' interpretation of the Sabbath, or even his prohibition of oaths and divorce, for it strikes at that which makes a Jew a Jew, and not merely an ethical monotheist. Or, to express it in a more positive way, if there is to be a bond of cohesion for God's people, Jesus taught that it must rest on something other than outward observance of the Law. It will be difficult, accordingly, to know who is a Jew in good standing and who is not.

Did Jesus mean to go as far as this? Jewish scholars are often inclined to doubt it. Does he not mean, "Internal cleanliness is more important than external"? Such would be the teaching of many Pharisaic rabbis who held, nevertheless, that the purity laws were binding. The great Johanan ben Zakkai even went so far as to say, "The dead body does not really defile, nor does water cleanse, but God has said, 'I have made an ordinance, I have promulgated a decree.'" Such a reduced interpretation of Luke 11:39-41 fits with Hebraic ways of speech. When Hosea said, "I desire mercy and not sacrifice" (Hos. 6:6) he may well have meant "I consider mercy more important than sacrifice."

If we can assume that some of our Lord's later followers understood him in just this way, the Church's first great internal controversy becomes easier to explain and understand. Later Jewish Christians in Palestine and Syria, perhaps even in Galilee itself, remained true to the ceremonial law. According to Jerome, there were such persons as late as the fourth century. The Book of Acts speaks of believers in Christ who belonged to the Pharisaic party (15:5) and of "myriads" who although they believe are yet "zealous for the Law" (21:20). Paul himself is pictured as claiming to be a Pharisee (23:6) and not merely a former one. It is easier to understand the controversy between Paul and the Hellenists, on the one hand, and the Christian Pharisees on the other, if we assume that both the parties could, with some plausibility, appeal to the historic Jesus. Conservative Jews rested on the known fact that, even if Jesus had modified the Law, he had remained true to it. There is nothing to suggest that he ate pork or did a full day's work on the Sabbath. Though he prophesied that the Temple would be destroyed, he spoke no word against the sacrificial system as such, but acted only against abuses which were corrupting it.

The radicals who opened the door of the Church to the Gentiles—and Paul was not the only one of these—insisted on the logical results of their Lord's teachings. He had not only shown great independence in his attitude to the Sabbath, oaths and divorce; he had undoubtedly eaten untithed foods and from vessels that were not ritually pure, and in a well-known saying he had relegated the purity laws to a place of minor importance. If a man is made clean or foul by the dispositions of his mind, if the only impurity is in the ethical realm, then in time of great need the purity laws must give way. And when, at a later time, Gentiles were drawn to the Kingdom of God, what could this be but a clear sign that God cared nothing about these externals? Was not the admission of Gentiles the logical application of Jesus' teaching about the clean and the unclean? The story of Peter's acceptance of Cornelius (Acts 10:1-35) is a dramatic illustration of the point.

If Jesus practically set aside the purity laws, did he not go in the direction opposite to sectarianism and virtually disregard the difference between Jew and Gentile? Could he have been influenced by contact with non-Jews—Gentiles and Samaritans?

He certainly had Gentile neighbors. Matthew is the only evangelist to preserve the command "Do not go on any road of the Gentiles, and into a city of the Samaritans do not enter" (Matt. 10:5)—and I must confess that it is impossible for me to understand this as a genuine saying of Jesus. From Nazareth the road led north to Sepphoris; the road southeast to Scythopolis, the ancient Beth-shan. Roads from Capernaum went to Tiberias, Hippos and Damascus.

It is perhaps impossible to discover the whole truth about relations between Jews and Gentiles in first-century Palestine. Up to recent years we have been almost completely dependent upon written sources, principally the rabbinic literature which reflects the convictions of religious experts who were, after all, Pharisees in their outlook. But for some time archaeological evidence has been piling up— remains of synagogues with their carvings and mosaic pavements, tombs, ossuaries, sarcophagi, lamps, glass and pottery vessels—in fact, all the physical remains of culture which must be taken into consideration but are so difficult to evaluate. One might suppose that, because of the biblical law against molten and graven images the Jews were as strict as later Moslems in avoiding pictures of human beings and animals, if it were not for the evidence from the second, third and later centuries of our era. But these remains show that in their use of art forms the Jews of Palestine shared in the oriental and Graeco-Roman culture about them. They did not scruple to use pictures and sym-

bols from pagan mythology in their tombs and even in
their synagogues. This is particularly true in Galilee, the
later stronghold of Pharisaism. How much of this is mere
decoration, and whether any of it represents the actual
influence of pagan thought, no one can surely say. But
the evidence, which runs to hundreds of items, completely
destroys the idea that the Jews—even in Palestine—formed
a cultural and religious island completely separated from
outside influence.

Therefore one must seriously ask what the gospels tell
us about Jesus in his relation to non-Jews. The older tradition shows him in only occasional, but friendly, relation
with Gentiles. Both Matthew and Luke locate in Capernaum the story of the centurion, whose faith he praised as
greater than any that he had found in Israel (Matt.
8:5-13=Luke 7:1-10). The story of the Syrophoenician
woman, which Mark places in the regions of Tyre, may
mark a development in Jesus' conception of his ministry.
It is only after some hesitation that he heals the woman's
daughter, but the woman nevertheless is commended for
her faith. A third story is the healing of the demoniac at
Gergesa, probably on the eastern shore of the Galilean
lake. These are sparse references, but significant. It would
have suited well the purposes of the evangelists if they
could have pictured a more extensive ministry to Gentiles,
but they manufactured no new stories and Mark preserved
the story of the Syrophoenician woman despite the difficult
saying it contains—"It is not right to take the children's
bread and cast it to dogs."

Matthew's special tradition makes the story more difficult by including the saying, "I have been sent only to the
lost sheep of the house of Israel" (Matt. 15:21). But, as
Frederick Grant has pointed out, this is a floating saying

whose emphasis was originally on lost sheep, not on Israel.[3] Jesus was sent only to those who were lost, not to those fenced inside the fold.

Finally, there is the bitter saying that it will be more tolerable at the day of judgment for Sodom and Gomorrah than for Chorazin, Bethsaida and Capernaum (Matt. 11:20-24=Luke 10:13-15). Not only has Jesus met with opposition from his own people and in the principal towns of his ministry; he sees them as having no special privileges on judgment day. On the contrary, because they have had an opportunity not given to others, they will be judged the more severely.

Jewish scholars have pointed out another element in the tradition which seems to them quite un-Jewish. This is the controversy over the casting out of demons through Beelzebul (Luke 11:14-23; cf. Mark 3:22-30=Matt. 12:22-32). For one thing, this throws light on the suspicions of Jesus' opponents. Beelzebul was an ancient Syrian deity. The name meets us first in the Ras Shamra texts of the fifteenth century B.C. It means "lord of the house," i.e. of the Temple, and is one of the titles of Aleyan Baal, a god of the Canaanite pantheon. In Old Testament times he is known as the god of Ekron, though the author of I Kings changes his name to Baal-zebub ("lord of flies") to show his contempt. In first-century Galilee he is apparently a minor pagan deity whom the Jews regarded as no more than a demon. The scribes suppose that, since Jesus is a Galilean, he is under pagan influence.

What surprises Jewish scholars is that in this controversy story Jesus seems tacitly to accept the concept of two

[3] F. C. Grant, *The Gospel of Matthew*, "Harper's Annotated Bible," No. 11 (New York, 1955), II, p. 11.

opposing kingdoms, the Kingdom of God and the Kingdom of Satan; rabbinical literature, they argue, ascribes no such importance to the demons. But the rabbinical writings are not a perfect mirror of first-century Judaism. The non-canonical apocalypses, which have long been known and studied, portray a regular hierarchy of evil spirits. The realm of evil is so prominent in the Dead Sea literature that one can draw a number of parallels between it and the Zoroastrian writings.

Early Christian literature goes much further in this direction than does Jesus. In Luke 4:6, when the devil offers Jesus authority over all the kingdoms of the world, the evangelist adds the words, "because it has been given over to me, and to whomever I wish I give it." Another clear reflection of early Christian belief is found in Codex W, the Freer manuscript, which contains an interpolation after Mark 16:14. Here the apostles say to Jesus that the present age is under Satan; whereupon Jesus is made to answer, "The limit of the years of Satan's authority has been completed, but other dreadful things draw near. . . ." This is not, however, the viewpoint of Jesus. But how far does he go?

One can, of course, say that in the story of the Beelzebul controversy he is arguing from the premises of his opponents. Yet the fact remains that Jesus sees the events of his ministry as the decisive battle between God's forces and the forces of evil. He therefore ascribes to evil some objective existence and personifies it. When the disciples return after having cast out demons, he says, "I was watching Satan fallen like lightning from heaven" (Luke 10: 18). He lived, after all, on the border of pagan lands whose people believed in Beelzebul, where both Jews and Gentiles fell under Beelzebul's spell or ascribed their miseries to him.

Jesus had no false optimism; he was acutely conscious of the power of evil—in men's illness and also in their sins and hatreds, and perhaps even in the political and social forces that were beyond their control. If ever he went to the top of a mountain like Tabor, he could see something of the kingdoms of the world and their glory and understand the helplessness and frustration which the sensitive man feels in the presence of vast concentrations of power. This may help to account for his recognition, in some way, of a Kingdom of Satan. But we must never forget that he believed that God was bringing this kingdom to an end. He is conscious of the power of God and he proclaims the Good News in full expectation that a large number of his countrymen will accept it and come into the Kingdom of God.

There was some contact, then, between Jesus and the Gentiles. Did he, in addition, carry on a ministry among the Samaritans?

An answer to this question should start from the story of the Samaritan mission in Acts. In Acts there is no indication that the gospel was preached in Samaria until after the martyrdom of Stephen, when the persecution scattered the believers through Judaea and Samaria "with the exception of the apostles" (Acts 8:1). Philip is the first evangelist of the region (8:5) and "the apostles" give their formal approval of the new step by sending Peter and John at a later time to lay hands on the new converts (8:14-16). This story reflects the viewpoint of Acts that the Jerusalem apostles exercised a certain control over the whole missionary enterprise and it may contain a memory of serious doubts as to the propriety of the new mission. After all, the Jerusalem tradition of Matthew contained a purported word of Jesus forbidding contact with the Samaritans.

The Gospel of John, in direct contradiction to this, tells of a dramatically successful ministry of Jesus in Samaritan territory. Here he is represented as setting aside the rival claims of Jerusalem and Mt. Gerizim; God's Temple is no longer to be localized, for the true worshippers, wherever they are, shall worship the Father in spirit and in truth (John 4:23). The late Professor Bacon was surely correct in calling this gospel "the Gospel of the Hellenists," for its teaching is the logical outcome of the work of Stephen and the prophets who founded the church in Antioch. The evangelist may well have these pioneers in mind when he says, "Others have labored, and you have entered into their labors" (4:38). As a result of Philip's work there is now a flourishing church in the Samaritan region. The fourth chapter of John reads the Samaritan mission back into the earthly ministry of Jesus and it is hard to tell how much historical basis exists for its tradition.

It is, however, probable that Jesus made a trip through Samaria. This becomes evident from a brief review of what the four gospels say about his movements. Mark begins his story with Jesus in the Jordan valley, being baptized by John. After the Baptist's arrest he comes into Galilee, proclaiming the Good News, and there he remains until his journey to Jerusalem, except that he makes one tour into Gentile territory to the northwest and northeast. When he leaves for Jerusalem his trip takes him east of the Jordan. He evidently crosses the river near Jericho and from Jericho comes up to the Holy City. Matthew adds nothing to this framework.

John, like Mark, begins with Jesus in the Jordan valley. But before John is cast into prison, our Lord goes to Gali-

lee and begins his work there (1:43–2:12). Then follows
the cleansing of the Temple in Jerusalem, an incident so
surprising at this point that Bacon believed it had been
inserted by a redactor. If the Fourth Evangelist had an old
account of Jesus' movements he may have interrupted
its sequence and, for theological reasons, placed the Cleansing there. The proof that the story is intruded is that in
3:22 we are told that Jesus goes into Judaea, as though he
were not already there. He remains in Judaea until 4:3.
John is baptizing at Aenon near Salim, but Jesus' work
outstrips that of the forerunner. At some time after this
point, the evangelist must have placed the imprisonment
of John.

Jesus now goes through Samaria (4:4-42) and into
Galilee. This period in Galilee is related in 4:43-54 and
chapter 6. Chapter 5 is out of place, as many commentators
have seen, and should come after chapter 6. In the fifth
chapter, Jesus now goes down to Jerusalem for a festival,
presumably Pentecost, and here arises the first bitter controversy with his Judaean opponents. There is no record
of a trip back to Galilee, but he is found there at the
beginning of chapter 7. Now he returns to Jerusalem for
the feast of Tabernacles and apparently stays there through
the feast of Dedication. There is no record of a separate
trip, and 10:1-21 serves as a transition between the two
festivals. He does not leave Judaea again except for an
interlude of work on the other side of the Jordan, where
John had baptized. He returns to Judea and is at Bethany until he goes to Jerusalem for the final Passover.

The situation in Luke is curious. The third evangelist
puts the early ministry in Galilee and, like Mark, brings
Jesus to Jerusalem only once. But instead of accepting the
route down the east side of Jordan, he says that Jesus began

his trip to Jerusalem with a visit to a "village of Samaritans" where he was repulsed (9:52-53). In succeeding chapters Luke includes a rich store of teaching material, including—interestingly enough—the parable of the Good Samaritan (10:30-37). At one time he indicates artistically the passage of time and continuance of the journey: "he was going through one city and village after another teaching and making his way to Jerusalem" (13:22). The next indication of locality is in 17:11, "And it happened that while he was going to Jerusalem he went through the midst of [or, between] Samaria and Galilee." This ought to mean that Jesus was on the border between the two territories, possibly somewhere near the modern Jenin. The incident of the thankful Samaritan, healed of leprosy, follows immediately. Other teachings follow, and then in 18:35 we suddenly find Jesus about to enter Jericho. Eight chapters have been filled with teaching material between the first resolution to go to the Holy City and the arrival at Jericho.

Professor C. C. McCown accounts for this curious situation by supposing that Luke knew very little Palestinian geography except for the road between Caesarea (Strato's Tower) on the seacoast and Jerusalem, which he had probably travelled; his geographical notices would therefore be a literary device to indicate a Samaritan ministry. In any case, Luke's account cannot be harmonized with those of Mark and John. A reader who was unacquainted with the other gospels would naturally suppose that Jesus kept on the west side of Jordan all the way; and there were in fact Roman roads from Scythopolis (Bethshan) to Jericho, and from Samaria to Jericho.

However artificial the geography of the gospels, however fragmentary the topographical traditions in them, both Luke and John seem to preserve some memory of a trip through Samaria. Furthermore, the evidence indicates that Jesus had made at least one trip to Jerusalem in addition to the one recounted in Mark. John contains some miracle stories whose scene is in Jerusalem, notably the healing at Bethesda which shows an exact knowledge of local topography; and some of Luke's sayings material (particularly 13:1-9) would fit well in Jerusalem. Finally, in Mark there are indications that Jesus spent more than one week in the Holy City. The Hosanna ritual at the triumphal entry fits Tabernacles or Dedication better than Passover. Jesus knows where an ass will be tied in the street, and arrangements have been made for an upper room for the Passover (11:2; 14:13-15). If Jesus visited Jerusalem more than once, it is probable that he made a trip through Samaria.

The conclusion is that Jesus sometimes came into contact with Samaritans. What actually were his relations with them? The story in Luke 9:52-56 says that when the Samaritans would not receive them, Jesus rebuked the brothers who wished to call down fire on them, "and they went into another village." This forbearing attitude is quite in character. Twice in the central section of Luke a Samaritan is the hero. Only the Samaritan leper returns to give thanks (17:16). The story has one peculiarity, for Jesus has expressly ordered the ten to show themselves to the priests, but this does not change the main point that Luke is trying to convey. The story is a counterpart to the famous parable of the Good Samaritan (10:25-37). There were rabbinic stories in which the three figures were priest, Levite and Israelite; the first two are shown as failing to fulfil their religious obligations, while the Israelite—that is, the ordinary layman—does the will of God. One can imagine that when Jesus begins the story his hearers expect the usual conclusion, but the hero turns out to be a member of the hated race.

Jewish rejection of contact with Samaritans was not absolute or universal. But how bitter the feeling was can be seen from the saying ascribed to Rabbi Eliezer, "He who eats the bread of the Samaritans is as one who eats the flesh of swine" (Mishnah, Shebiith 8:10). Israelites at a later time were forbidden to marry Samaritans, and many provisions of rabbinic law treat Samaritans as if they were Gentiles. As early as the beginning of the second century B.C. Jeshua ben Sira says, "With two nations is my soul vexed, and the third is no nation: they that sit upon the mountain of Samaria, and the Philistines, and that foolish people that dwelleth at Sichem" (Ecclus. 50:25-26).

Jesus' parable, therefore, implies a bitter rebuke on the Jews for their attitude toward a people who were so similar to them but just different enough to inspire feelings of hatred and contempt. He obviously recognized that there were Samaritans who, like the Gentile centurion of Capernaum, put Jews to shame by their faith and behavior. It would not be surprising if there is some historical basis for the story of his meeting with the Samaritan woman.

For many reasons, then, we must agree that Jesus was not in every way a typical Jew. The difference between Jews and Samaritans, or between Jews and Gentiles, does not have the same significance to him as to the Jerusalem Pharisees. But is this due to some influence of Gentile thought on his mind?

According to all our sources, he spent practically all his time with his own people, and only occasionally came into contact with Gentiles and Samaritans. This is very remarkable, since at least three of our gospels were written by Gentiles who take every opportunity to emphasize his good will toward non-Jews. If Jesus had talked or thought like a Greek, Mark and Luke might have seized on that fact with great satisfaction. But there is no trace of Greek philosophy in his teaching, or of pagan thought unless the belief in Beelzebul is such; and Beelzebul is for him not a god but a demon whose end is in sight. Nor is there any sign that Jesus hoped to bring peace in Galilee between Jew and Gentile through closer intercourse between the nations. It is rather that he approaches the problem of the Jew and the member of another nation as he does the controversies over the Law, in the same simple, direct, non-technical way. While firmly rooted in the religion of his own people, Jesus' fundamental attitude toward Jews and Gentiles is the same. As human beings, all stand equally under the judgment and mercy of God. Even the written Law must give way before this all-embracing conviction. The logical and inevitable outcome of his attitude is a universal Church for all nations. While Jesus never deserted his nation, he said and did that which rendered a new Church inevitable. His opponents seem to have been conscious of the revolutionary implications of his teaching; therefore they rejected him.

CHAPTER VII

JESUS AND THE
REVOLUTIONISTS

MOST ancient histories have been written from the viewpoint of scholars interested in classical Greek and Roman civilization. One who would understand the disturbed emotional climate of the first century in Palestine must, however, look at Roman history with the eyes of a Near Easterner. The Jews were an ancient and proud nation. Their sacred books commanded the respect of Greeks and Romans; among the Mediterranean peoples, only the Egyptians had traditions of such antiquity. By comparison, the Romans were parvenus. Furthermore, these sacred books assigned to Israel an absolutely unique rôle in world history. The Jew looked back to the time when God had directly created the nation by bringing the tribes out of Egypt. He also remembered the days of David and Solomon when, thanks to the weakness of Mesopotamia and Egypt, the kingdom's borders had expanded, and this period was idealized as the pattern of the future. But Israel's lot was something more than political empire, for the rabbis taught that while God created all the nations of the earth, only Israel had accepted his Law. A covenant had been made with this Chosen People; and however unfaithful they had been from time to time, they were chosen, and God would not forsake his covenant with them. A time was coming when God's reign would be revealed. At this time sin would disappear from Israel so that the holy people might be fit for their manifest destiny. Jerusalem would then be the center of the earth, and God's dominion would be exercised through the saints of the Most High. From this point of view—which all religious Jews seem to have taken for granted—the future of Israel was an essential part of religious faith, the only true faith in the world.

Apocalyptic literature contains many variations on this theme. The Hebrew Bible includes some of these writings, most notably Daniel and the latter part of Zechariah. Most of them—the Testaments of the Twelve Patriarchs, Enoch, the Psalms of Solomon, the Apocalypse of Baruch, and so on—never attained the official acceptance for which their writers must have hoped. The recently discovered Dead Sea writings have apocalyptic features. In some books the future age is to be brought by a Messiah or anointed king, usually a descendant of David but occasionally from the tribe of Levi, while in others God himself will bring the new age directly, without any human intermediary. Sometimes the golden age, while it is miraculous, is frankly a continuation of this present earth and its conditions; at other times it is pictured as like heaven or the Garden of Eden. But all of these writings agree in making Israel God's agent in ruling what is essentially a world-empire, however religious and ethical it may be, and most of them predict that the new order will be set up only after a great war in which the Jewish people are victorious.

Jewish faith was shaken to its foundations in the years 169-167 B.C. when Antiochus IV Epiphanes, Seleucid monarch of Syria and overlord of Palestine, tried to stamp out the religion. The trouble arose partly from Antiochus' desire to establish a uniform Greek culture in his realm and partly from party strife among the Jews. At this time most

Jews were devoted to their ancestral customs and their political sympathies were with Egypt, which had ruled them before 198 B.C. when Antiochus III conquered Palestine. There was, however, a pro-Syrian minority, enthusiastic for Greek culture. On his accession, Antiochus IV appointed as high priest a man named Joshua (who took the Greek name Jason) and the Hellenizing program proceeded rapidly. But Jason was outbid and soon replaced by another aspirant to the high priestly office, Menahem or Menelaus, who turned the Temple treasures over to the Syrian monarch. When civil war arose in Jerusalem, Antiochus IV descended on the city, set up an altar to the Olympian Zeus on the place of burnt offerings, and sacrificed swine there.

All Jewish religious observances were now forbidden. Even possession of a scroll of the Law was punishable by death. The Syrian king demanded worship of heathen gods. This is very possibly the first strictly *religious* persecution that the Jews had ever experienced.

To this there were two characteristic Jewish responses. One is represented by the Book of Daniel, a tract written on this occasion. The teaching of this is that the pride of man will be humbled and only the Lord exalted. God has punished the Jews for their many sins and that the restoration of political independence and true worship can come about only from God's action and not that of man. All that the loyal Jew can do is to witness for his faith, to endure persecution, even to death, and trust in God.

The other response is reflected in the Books of Maccabees. A small group, under the leadership of Judas Maccabaeus, decided to resist and fight. It is significant that First Maccabees, our best source for the events of these years, has practically nothing to say about religion. The

Maccabees were not anti-religious—they wished to preserve ancestral customs—but they relied entirely on their
own efforts. The *hasidim* or pious, to whom the Book of
Daniel belongs, were distrustful of the Maccabean program. In succeeding years Judas Maccabaeus and his
brothers gained a measure of independence, finally the
Maccabean rulers took the title of king, and a Jewish state
continued until Pompey the Great put an end to it in
63 B.C.

During this century of Jewish monarchy the gulf between the *hasidim* and the Maccabees widened. The Pharisaic party, most of whose members were pacifists and
quietists, was the principal development out of the hasidic
movement. The Essenes were another. So were the authors
of the many apocalypses. This indicates that, as one might
expect, the movement for the restoration of Jewish religion
had many varieties and ramifications. Although most
Pharisees asked nothing more than freedom to practice
the Law, others who adopted the legal ideas of Pharisaism
were nevertheless ready to fight for independence. When,
later on, Herod the Great set up a golden eagle over the
entrance to his new Temple in Jerusalem, a group of young
men, incited by a pair of strict and fanatical rabbis, cut
it down. Josephus the historian, who was one of the
generals at the time of the revolt in A.D. 66-70, claimed
to be a Pharisee; and Rabbi Aqiba, one of the greatest
figures in Jewish religious history, supported the independence movement of Simeon bar Koziba (or bar
Kokhba) in A.D. 132.

All this is just what we ought to expect. Hardly ever
in history has there been a religious sect or party whose
members were in perfect agreement on every ethical principle. In fact, members of a worshipping group are often

divided in politics. Even pacifist churches have non-pacifist members. It would be a mistake, therefore, to suppose that the revolutionists were non-religious; or to say that merely because a man was an apocalyptist he would not fight. The faith of an individual often contains very diverse elements.

Among the Dead Sea scrolls we have an actual document written as a guide for carrying on a holy war. The so-called *War Scroll* or *Rule of Battle for the Children of Light* is a curious combination of tactics and liturgics. The "children of light" for whom it is written appear to represent the tribes of Levi, Judah and Benjamin; the "children of darkness" are Edom, Moab, Ammon, Philistia and "the Kittim of Asshur." Many students identify these last with the Seleucid Greeks of Syria and date the scroll in the Maccabean period.

The book prescribes the organization of the Jewish army, the battle flags to be carried, the trumpet calls to be sounded by priests and Levites at various points in the battle, the priests' prayers, the hymn of thanksgiving after battle, and the bathing and washing of clothing by which the soldiers afterward purify themselves. The great banner which goes before the entire army bears the motto "People of El" (God); the company banner reads "From God comes the force of battle against all wicked flesh"; the flag of the squad, "Joyful praises with the harp to God."

What group is responsible for the *War Scroll?* The extreme emphasis on religion and priestly leadership makes it unlikely that the book represents Judas Maccabaeus and his men. The prayers and hymns are full of quotations from the Book of Isaiah, particularly its last and most nationalistic parts, and Isaiah was one of the favorite books of the Qumran sect. Even if the members of this order were not directly engaged in revolt in the first century, some of their predecessors must have planned a holy war, and the book was carefully preserved as part of their literature.

Between the death of Herod the Great in 4 B.C. and the outbreak of the Jewish War in A.D. 66, a continual procession of revolutionists marches across the pages of Palestinian history. The rioters who cut down Herod's golden eagle were not forgotten. Memory of their martyrdom kept the Judaean extremists stirred up. Archelaus, who succeeded his father Herod and took the title of ethnarch or ruler of the nation, at first tried to placate his subjects, but a riot in the Temple at Passover time led him to send troops who butchered people as they offered their sacrifices. Seven weeks later, at Pentecost, Jewish mobs seized the Temple and hippodrome and besieged the royal palace. A brigand chief broke open the arsenal at Sepphoris in Galilee and armed his followers. A royal slave named Simon assumed the diadem in Transjordan and burned the palaces at Jericho and Betharamatha. Athrongaeus, a shepherd, led another insurrection in which he and his men surrounded a Roman century at Emmaus, the modern Amwas. It required the intervention of Roman troops under Varus to restore peace, and Varus is said to have crucified two thousand Jews.

Ten years of this unrest were enough. Augustus removed Archelaus from office in A.D. 6, to the great relief of the moderate elements, and annexed Judaea as a small imperial province under a procurator or financial officer named Coponius. The new organization rendered a census and financial survey desirable and Quirinius, legate of Syria, came to Judaea for that purpose. This was the signal for a new outbreak. Though their leaders persuaded the

Judaean Jews to submit, a man known as Judas the Galilean, who came from Gamala in Gaulonitis, northeast of the Sea of Galilee, began a revolt. Josephus credits to him and his associate, the Pharisee Sadduk, the formation of a fourth "philosophy" or party. This group is said to have agreed with the other Pharisees in everything except that it was fanatically devoted to national independence. No man could be called ruler or Lord; this prerogative belonged to God alone. Taxation was only the first step toward slavery; the nation must assert its liberty, and God would surely help the Jews if they dared to take matters into their own hands. Judas taught his followers to despise torture and death. Many years later the Stoic philosopher Epictetus speaks of the Galileans and their freedom from fear of tyrants, and it is not certain whether he means Christians or the followers of men like Judas.

Certainly this was not mere nationalism but the strictest idea of theocracy. Whatever the origin of the *War Scroll,* it illustrates the temper of mind of Judas the Galilean.

Tiberius came to the imperial throne in A.D. 14. As a matter of imperial policy he kept his provincial governors in office for long terms. Every proconsul and legate got rich in a short while; so, no doubt, did the procurators who ruled smaller areas. The oftener the change took place, the more the provinces were milked of revenue; and Tiberius wanted the empire to be prosperous. Under his first procurator of Judaea, Valerius Gratus, there seems to have been peace. The second was Pontius Pilate. Pilate, whose term was approximately A.D. 26-36, began his administration with a serious blunder: when he introduced his troops he neglected to remove from the military standards the *semaiai* or medallions that bore the emperor's picture and which at least at a later period were worshipped by the legionaries. In the Holy Land this was idolatry, and Pilate was finally forced to bow to Jewish scruples.

Jerusalem has never had a completely adequate water supply, and Pilate undertook to remedy this by building an aqueduct fifty Roman miles in length. To meet the cost he seized the sacred treasure of the Temple, the result was a demonstration, and Pilate sent soldiers in civilian dress who beat many of the rioters to death. The last incident of his governorship began when a crowd of excitable Samaritans marched toward Mount Gerizim to find sacred vessels which Moses was believed to have hidden there. Apparently fearing an uprising, Pilate sent troops to massacre this mob. Vitellius, legate of Syria, then ordered Pilate to Rome and redressed some of the grievances of both Jews and Samaritans. Tiberius upheld Vitellius and dismissed Pilate, who now disappears from history.

The reign of the emperor Gaius Caligula (A.D. 37-41) was a period of crisis for the Jewish people. Accusations against the Jews of Alexandria made it necessary for the great philosopher Philo to visit Rome and defend his compatriots. Previous emperors had permitted worship of themselves in the Near East, but Caligula actively promoted it. When Petronius, legate of Syria, received orders to have the statues of the emperor set up in the sanctuary at Jerusalem, it seemed to Palestinian Jews to be a repetition of the days of Antiochus Epiphanes. Petronius marched an army of at least two legions toward Judaea. A large number of Jews met him at Ptolemais, the modern Acre, and begged the legate not to carry out the order. Petronius went to Galilee and summoned the notables of the country to Tiberias. There he was told that in order to execute the emperor's decree he would have to sacrifice the entire nation; and, according to Josephus, the Jews then present offered themselves, their wives and children, to be slaughtered.

Palestinian Christians felt the tragic danger as keenly as did other Jews. To them the imperial statue in the Temple would be nothing less than "the abomination that makes desolate" mentioned in Daniel 11:31; 12:11, a clear sign of the end of the age. Most New Testament scholars regard Mark 13:14-19 as part of a Christian apocalypse written at this time, i.e. about A.D. 40. Fortunately, Petronius decided to appeal to Caligula; still more fortunately, news of the murder of Caligula reached him before he received the emperor's letter threatening him with death.

The accession of Claudius (41-54) meant better days for the Jews of Palestine, for the entire country was made a kingdom under Herod Agrippa I, grandson of Herod the Great, who was scrupulous in observance of the Jewish Law. Christians, the Book of Acts tells us, were persecuted during the brief reign of this popular prince. James, the son of Zebedee, was put to the sword and Peter imprisoned (Acts 12:1-3).

A papyrus found in 1924 supplements the stories of Josephus and the Book of Acts at one point. This is a letter written by the emperor Claudius to Alexandria in the first year of his reign.[1] Here the Jews are forbidden to intrude into certain athletic contests and to send two separate embassies (presumably to Rome), but are bidden to enjoy the prosperity and privileges which they have in Alexandria. They are also warned "not to introduce or invite Jews who sail down from Syria to Egypt, thus compelling me to conceive the greater suspicion." It has been

---

[1] H. Idris Bell, *Jews and Christians in Egypt* (London, 1924), esp. pp. 28-29.

suggested that one of the two Jewish embassies was Jewish Christian, and that therefore in Alexandria and perhaps elsewhere in the Jewish world there were disorders between Christians and other Jews. However this may be, the situation was serious enough that Claudius did not want Syrian Jews to come to Egypt.

We may remind ourselves that both Acts and the Roman biographer Suetonius tell of Claudius expelling the Jews from Rome—most probably about the year 49, though some scholars would date the event much earlier. Suetonius adds that the tumult which led to their exile had Chrestus (Christ? the Messiah?) as its instigator (*impulsore Chresto*). This may point to Messianic outbreaks, whether or not Christians were involved. At any rate, Prisca and Aquila, known to us from both Acts and the letters of Paul, were among the Jews who left Rome.

Thus there had been recurrent disorders all through the decade from 4 B.C. to A.D. 6 and for several years thereafter; again in Pilate's procuratorship; and at least the threat of trouble in the year 40 and thereafter. After the death of Agrippa I (A.D. 44) the country was again ruled by procurators. The first of these, Cuspius Fadus (about 44-46), had to deal with a Jewish attack on the inhabitants of Philadelphia, the modern Amman, capital of the Hashemite Kingdom of Jordan. He also captured a bandit named Tholomy who had ravaged Idumaea in the south, and Theudas, the revolutionist mentioned in Acts 5:36.

Theudas' movement seems to have had a religious character. According to Acts "he said that he himself was someone," an indication that he claimed to be a prophet or Messianic king; Josephus tells that he led the people to the Jordan river and promised that (like Joshua) he would divide its waters to give them passage through.

Next on the scene were the sons of Judas the Galilean. These were crucified by Fadus' successor, Tiberius Alexander, a paganized Jew. This must have been about the time of the famine in Palestine when Christians were sending relief to the church in Jerusalem.

Some time in the period from 48 to 52, when Ventidius Cumanus was procurator, an incident occurred at Passover time. A Roman cohort was stationed as usual on the roof of the Temple portico, and an obscene insult offered by one of the soldiers led to a riot. Reinforcements were sent in, and, according to Josephus, at least 20,000 Jews were crushed to death. Even if allowances are made for exaggeration in numbers, the slaughter must have been immense. Cumanus' administration saw the rise of another bandit leader named Eleazar who maintained himself for some years until the procurator Felix captured him.

Under Felix (usually dated 52-60) the nationalist movement entered another phase. Bands of *sicarii* or dagger-bearing assassins penetrated crowds at festival times and slew Romans and their supporters. Prophets, claiming divine inspiration, led groups of people out into the desert, promising that God would give them "signs of freedom." One of these, an Egyptian, led a huge crowd to the Mount of Olives, planning to attack Jerusalem, but prompt action by Felix ended the revolt. This man, like several of the other revolutionists, is mentioned in Acts (21:38). Tension increased in the time of Festus (about 60-62). Although he captured a number of guerrilla leaders, the sicarii became more numerous. The last two procurators, Albinus and Gessius Florus, were, from all accounts, worse than any of their predecessors. Brutal and unable to understand their subjects or to deal with them, they apparently goaded them to revolt. With the inevitability of a Greek tragedy, the

Jewish War came on. Beginning in 66, it dragged on until in August of the year 70 the Temple fell in flames. When the last resistance was finally crushed under Titus, the Jewish people had undergone the greatest slaughter in their long and sad history.

The story just told is fragmentary. Practically all of it comes from the pages of Josephus, who was dependent on earlier historians for the events in the earlier part of the first century. But we know enough to realize that Jesus' boyhood was lived in an atmosphere of turmoil and revolution. Small wonder that the evangelist Luke includes in the infancy stories hymns that proclaim:

> He has scattered those who in the thought of their heart are arrogant;
> He has taken down potentates from their thrones and exalted the lowly;
> The hungry he has filled with good things and the rich he has sent away empty (*Magnificat*, Luke 1:51-53).
> The oath which he swore to our father Abraham, that he would grant us
> That having been rescued from the hand of our enemies
> We should serve him without fear in purity and righteousness
> In his presence all our days (*Benedictus*, 1:73-75).

The sources are abundant enough, too, to disclose the extraordinary mosaic which constituted Palestinian life: Greek cities such as Ptolemais, Caesarea, Sepphoris, Sebaste (Samaria); Gadara, Gerasa and other towns of the Decapolis, inhabited by Romans and Hellenized Syrians, proud of their civic organization and rights and their relation to Rome; Jewish villages scattered here and there; the unassimilable Samaritans; Jerusalem, with its scholars and active intellectual life, the pilgrimage place for all Jews, always torn by political and religious factions; and the peasantry, both Jewish and pagan, whose immediate concern was getting a living from the land and keeping as much of the produce as possible.

The land was rich—more so than today, when deforestation has reduced the effectiveness of the rainfall—and the Jews were intelligent and energetic; but they were also prolific, and the country suffered from over-population. Frederick Grant, who has studied the economic situation carefully, points out that the Jews were under two systems of taxation, neither of which took the other into consideration. The Romans taxed crops, and also assessed import duties, sales taxes, poll taxes and highway and bridge tolls. Tithes, first-fruits, redemption money for the first-born, and the annual Temple tax were among the religious duties. Grant concludes that the tax burden in Judaea amounted to at least 30 or 40 per cent;[2] and this was an agricultural nation, not a modern state wealthy from industrial mass-production.

To the Roman government Palestine must have been an annoying and insoluble puzzle. It was not governed worse than other provinces, most of which were prosperous and even happy. It was not Rome's fault if the Jews insisted on paying religious taxes too; and the religious tenacity of the people was baffling to a pagan. The Jews, on their part, regarded the Romans as impious intruders, and in all probability civil taxation was heavier under the procurators than under Herod the Great. But, above all, it was the religious nationalism of the Jews that made them unhappy

[2] F. C. Grant, *The Economic Background of the Gospels* (New York and London, 1926), p. 105.

and desperate in their situation. Israel was God's own nation, with a great past and a glorious destiny; if Roman rule was to be endured at all, it was only for a time; there was no such thing as *Roma aeterna* in Jewish thinking.

The Book of Revelation illustrates the Semitic, Near Eastern temper of mind. It is written in the province of Asia, most of whose inhabitants were enthusiastically loyal to Rome. "The birth of the god [Augustus]," says an inscription from Priene about the beginning of our era, "was the beginning of good tidings for the inhabited world." But the author of Revelation, although he is a Christian, thinks like an oriental Jew. He does not see the prosperity, only the famines and the oppressive edicts regulating the planting of vines and grain. All the glory and luxury of Rome is built on human slavery. Rome is nothing more than Babylon, and God has promised that it will fall.

Some Palestinian Jews were passive and waited for God alone, by direct action, to bring in better days. But those who wanted action were offered two ways of salvation— religious observance and revolution. Most Pharisees seem to have taught that Israel's destiny was religious; the only important thing to do was to revitalize the nation's life by observing the Law. This meant that, while only God could solve the political problem, man nevertheless could do something. He had an outlet for his energies and emotions and the satisfaction of a rich life of distinctive culture, the true worship of the one God and an enduring social relationship. Jesus was not in complete disagreement with this. But instead of accepting the complicated Pharisaic program, he offered a non-technical—one might almost say lay—interpretation of the Law which made strict moral demands and called for a high degree of individual judgment and responsibility.

Jesus likewise rejected the way of revolution. Just what, then, was his attitude to government and political life? The answer to this question was of great importance to his followers; no doubt they were often urged to take part in the nationalist movement and perhaps some of them sympathized with it. Outsiders were interested too. What were the aims of a man who could command such a following? It was an important question regarding any rabbi or prophet, for religious men had influence with the people.

One looks in vain in Jesus' teaching for a clear indication of actual loyalty to any government. Civil obedience, yes; but not positive allegiance.

From shortly after his birth to the end of his life, Jesus was a subject of Herod Antipas, son of Herod the Great and tetrarch of Galilee and Peraea or Transjordan. This prince was never given the title of king or more troops than a police force. Yet he must have governed to the satisfaction of Rome until A.D. 39 when, out of jealousy toward Agrippa I, he demanded the royal dignity and Caligula banished him. He had first been married to a daughter of Aretas IV, king of Nabataean Arabia, but then he decided to marry Herodias, the wife of his half-brother. Aretas attacked him and destroyed his little army, but the emperor Tiberius protected Antipas and sent troops under Vitellius against the Arabian king.

This may have occurred some time after the death of John the Baptist. The Gospel of Mark says that Antipas had John beheaded because John denounced the unlawful marriage. According to Josephus, Antipas was more calculating. Disturbed by John's immense popularity and influence, he "thought it much better to execute him first, before any revolutionary movement should arise because of him, than to get himself into difficulties and regret, after it was too late, that he had not acted." Antipas appears in two other incidents in the Gospel of Luke. In the middle of the central section, certain Pharisees report to Jesus that Herod intends to kill him, and Jesus answers, "Go, tell that fox, 'See, I am casting out demons and carrying on healings today and tomorrow, and on the third day I shall be finished'" (Luke 13:31-32). At the time of Jesus' trial, Pilate is said to have sent him to Antipas as an act of courtesy to the latter. Herod then returned him to the procurator, and the result was a reconciliation between the two (Luke 23:6-12).

A group of "Herodians" is mentioned twice in the Gospel of Mark. They are presumably the partisans of the tetrarch; perhaps there had always been a group that backed the Herodian family. These two notices suggest that the government had its eye on the teacher from Nazareth. The Herodians are represented as plotting with the Pharisees to put Jesus to death (Mark 3:6); we do not know why. Together with the Pharisees, they also—according to Mark—try to trap him with the question of paying taxes to the emperor (Mark 12:13=Matt. 22:16). The scene is laid in Judaea, where imperial taxation was an immediate issue; one supposes that in Galilee taxes were paid, not to the emperor, but to the tetrarch. Galileans would, of course, have been vitally interested, for their land might at any time become a Roman province. Jesus' answer, "Pay the emperor what belongs to the emperor and pay God what belongs to God," agreed with the viewpoint of those Pharisees who refused to revolt against Rome. This was far from positive allegiance, and it does not mean that religion and the state occupy mutually exclusive realms. As every religious Jew—and particularly every Pharisee—would be quick to realize, God's Realm is all-inclusive and the emperor's sovereignty is subordinate. In case of a genuine conflict of loyalties, one must, as Peter said later, obey God rather than men (Acts 5:29). The emphasis in Jesus' saying is on man's duty to God, but at least he disclaimed any intention to defy the taxing authority which was then in power.

Another source, the material peculiar to Matthew, gives independent evidence that this was Jesus' attitude. The curious story of the stater in the fish's mouth (Matt. 17: 24-27) is concerned with the question whether the annual Temple tax of one half-shekel should be paid. Jesus asks Peter, "From whom do the kings of the earth receive duties and poll taxes? From their sons or from others?" When Peter answers, "From others," Jesus concludes, "Therefore the sons are free. But lest we cause them to stumble, go cast a hook into the sea and take the first fish that comes up, open its mouth and you will find a stater; take it and give it to them for me and you."

The story may have taken its present form before the destruction of the Temple, when the tax was actually paid to the priesthood in Jerusalem. After the year A.D. 70 the Roman government collected this poll tax from Jews and used the money for its own purposes, and many scholars think that this section in the gospel reflects the perplexity of Jewish Christians who wondered whether they were obliged to pay it. The exact origin of the story does not matter. The point is that the tradition represents Jesus as teaching that his followers are free sons of God—a position much like that of St. Paul—but that they must have consideration for others. Catch fish, carry on your regular occupation, pay the tax! The tax is relatively unimportant, and your scruples about it must not cause others to stumble, i.e. fall away from true service to God.

The gospels show, over and over again, that Jesus was acutely conscious of the political situation in Palestine. We have already referred to the Herodians and to the fact that he called Herod Antipas "that fox." Antipas is mentioned in another saying. In the midst of a confused section full of theological interpretation, the word stands out: "Beware of the leaven of the Pharisees and the leaven of Herod" (Mark 8:15). Readers of the gospels, because they are familiar with the parable of the leaven (Matt. 13:33 = Luke 13:20-21) are accustomed to think of yeast as a figure for the Kingdom of God. But in rabbinic literature, as in St. Paul's teaching (I Cor. 5:8), it represents wickedness—at Passover time every bit of it is thrown out of the house— and this is the obvious meaning here. The Pharisees and Herod are once more put together, this time as that which contaminates the whole lump.

Several of Jesus' parables contain the figure of a king. The king is always thought of as possessing absolute power; no one can question his judgments. Oftentimes the king is a figure of God, and in these instances he is a good king, even though strict and severe with those who make light of his graciousness. But in other places, where the king does not represent God, he is not an admirable character. For example, intertwined with Luke's parable of the pounds (Luke 19:12a, 13, 15-26) is a parable (19:12b, 14, 27) which tells of a man who went to a far country to receive a kingdom. But his citizens hated him and sent an embassy to say that they did not want him to rule them. On his return he had his enemies slain in his presence. This suggests that Jesus knew of the situation under Archelaus. A king wishes to go to war against another king and sits down to consider whether, with his ten thousand men, he dare meet a force of twenty thousand; he may decide to send an embassy and ask for peace (Luke 14:31-32). It is barely possible that here is a reference to Herod Antipas' disastrous war with Aretas—unless, of course, that took place after this time.

Jesus in fact has a certain scorn of royalty. "You know," he says, "that those who are supposed to rule over the Gentiles lord it over them, and their great ones exercise authority over them. But it shall not be so among you" (Mark 10:42-43). He draws an unforgettable contrast between the luxurious kings and John the Baptist, greatest of the prophets, who is a real man. "What did you go out to see? A man clothed in soft clothing? See! those who wear soft clothing are in the houses of kings!" (Matt. 11:8=Luke 7:25). One is reminded of the numerous sayings of rabbis in the first three centuries of our era who warn their followers to beware of the government. But it is more than this; the way of political power is rejected, not because it is certain to fail, not merely because the baubles of royalty are stupid, empty and contemptible, but because it is wrong. Not by accident does the story of Jesus' public ministry begin with his rejection of the temptation to possess the kingdoms of this world (Matt. 4:8-10=Luke 4:5-8). All of this helps to explain why Jesus is so reluctant to accept the title Messiah; its associations, for the first-century Jew, are more royal than religious.

Jesus is also conscious of the unrest in Palestine in the first century. The mysterious saying of Matt. 11:12 (cf. Luke 16:16) may mean that the revolutionists were seeking to establish the Kingdom of God by force: "From the days of John the Baptist until now the Kingdom of the Heavens suffers violence, and violent men seize it." On another occasion certain people tell him "of the Galileans whose blood Pilate mingled with their sacrifices" (Luke

13:1). Josephus tells of no such incident and the story sounds more like that of the massacre in Archelaus' time. Whatever the background, Jesus rejects the idea that the Galileans were especially great sinners and therefore had been punished. "No, I tell you, but unless you repent, you likewise will perish" (13:3). One of the parables tells of wicked farmers who kill first the slaves, and then the heir, in the hope of possessing the vineyard for themselves (Mark 12:1-9). Absentee ownership was common, and the Talmud tells of men who had lands in Judaea and Galilee, with a wife in each place. The figures in the parable are only incidental to the story, but the vengeance taken on the tenants, who resort to violence to get the vineyard, is at any rate used to illustrate the judgment of God.

The later Galilean followers of Jesus were pacifists and quietists. Much of our information about them comes from the church historian Hegesippus, whose book is lost except for quotations preserved by Eusebius in the fourth century. Hegesippus tells the story, somewhat legendary in its details but credible enough, of how the grandsons of Jude, the brother of the Lord, were brought before the emperor Domitian. These men acknowledged that they were descended from David, but said that the kingdom of Christ was not of the world or earthly, but heavenly and angelic, and would appear only at the end of the age (Eusebius H. E. iii. 20. 1-5). The same writer portrays James the brother of the Lord as a withdrawn holy man who spent all his time in prayer and supplication. James, as pictured here, resembles both the Essenes and the old saint Simeon portrayed in the Gospel of Luke.

The Jesus of the gospels is not withdrawn from ordinary life. On the contrary, he is on the open road, actively preaching and teaching. The evidence cited above shows, further, that he took a highly independent attitude toward the authorities, both political and religious, and, like the Old Testament prophets, was keenly aware of the political situation. On the other hand, while he believed that God alone was king, and men were his free children, he rejected the revolutionary movement entirely. The Sermon on the Mount contains added evidence in its sayings on anger, retaliation and love of enemies. These refer primarily to personal relationships, but they are sufficient in themselves to rule out the program of the zealots as impossible for the followers of Jesus.

Many farmers who live in a buffer state try to keep aloof from politics. They hope that, when the storms of war come, they will sweep over their fields and themselves without doing too much harm. In this reduced sense, the meek sometimes do inherit the earth. Galilee may have been the hotbed of revolution, but no doubt there were Galileans, both Jewish and pagan, who tried to preserve themselves by being neutral. Jesus was not one of these. Far from having any calculated program for peace and quiet, he counsels the love of enemies. This is sometimes dangerous, for it can be misunderstood as collaboration; indeed more than once Jesus predicts controversy and persecution as the result of his work. But the new rule for behavior is given without thought of consequences. It is simply God's way. God himself sends rain on the just and the unjust, and it is his will that man should imitate his loving-kindness.

Although Jesus rejected the way of violence, which his compatriots followed to their own destruction, he was actually crucified as a revolutionary. This is one of the great paradoxes of history. Perhaps the authorities feared him because they could not believe that a man with such a large popular following could have no political program.

· CHAPTER VIII ·

JESUS AND THE FUTURE HOPE

RELIGIOUS Jews in the first century, whatever their school of thought, believed that the future was in the hand of God. Man, as the instrument of God, had his subordinate part in bringing the future to pass. There were two ways by which the Jewish people might be saved—a revival of religion and a political restoration. In times of despair, however, all that man could do seemed inadequate, and the man of faith relied on the apocalyptic hope. God would shortly accomplish that which was beyond the power of man. We do not know whether large numbers of Palestinian Jews turned away from the two programs of action and tried to leave matters entirely in the hands of God. We know only that, from the time when Daniel was written, early in the Maccabean period, and at least till the end of the first century of our era, many apocalyptic books were composed.

Nearly all of these contain the type of prophecy found in Daniel; that is, the seer is presented as having lived in the far distant past. These books were written in the name of such men as Jeremiah's secretary Baruch, the sons of Jacob, and even Enoch, the seventh in Adam's line. In each case the ancient prophet looks into the future and tells of historical events in the years just prior to the time when the apocalypse was actually written. Past history is presented by symbols, with animals, angels and demons as the actors. For example, the various world empires appear in Daniel as four great beasts. After the temporary domination of the beast empires comes "one like a son of man," who symbolizes the human and humane rule of the saints of the Most High. This is the point at which prophecy of the past ceases and prophecy of the future begins. Nearly every apocalypse contains such a transition, after which the prophecy becomes more heavenly and miraculous. This is of course the time when the apocalyptist wrote the book, and a date can be assigned if the preceding historical notices are sufficiently clear.

Sometimes an apocalypse contains elaborate calculations of years, months and days. The thought behind this is that God has predestined the world's history with a definite time table. The apocalyptist calculates how many years or weeks of years have already elapsed, and then predicts how much time remains before the end. In the Book of Jubilees, which seems to have been used by the Dead Sea sect, this is connected with the idea of a year of 364 days and an insistence that the religious calendar conform to such a scheme. The Manual of Discipline speaks several times of the "proper reckoning of the time" and, without specifying when it will be, speaks of the last time, the season of the decreed judgment, when God's visitation is expected.

Early Christianity directly inherited much of this apoca·lyptic hope. One prominent part of the Gospel of Mark, the thirteenth chapter, draws on Daniel for the idea of an "abomination that makes desolate" and promises an early end to the troubles of God's people. "If the Lord had not shortened the days, no flesh would have been saved; but for the sake of the elect whom he chose he has shortened the days" (13:20). The letters of Paul, and above all the Book of Revelation, show how deeply early Christianity was influenced by this way of thinking.

Chapter 13 of Mark may contain some sayings of Jesus, but most of it does not fit with his other teachings; most historians regard it as an early Christian apocalypse. Yet other sayings of Jesus show that apocalyptic was part of the mental climate in which he lived. He did not ignore it; but how much of it did he accept?

Any attempt at an answer must start from his teaching about the Kingdom of God, for here we are on solid ground. There can be no doubt that one of the main themes of his preaching is God's Reign, and this is a concept drawn from the Old Testament.

Perhaps the best way to appreciate the Old Testament conception of God's Reign is to listen to the first part of Händel's *Messiah*. These scriptural passages, usually read in Christian churches in the Advent and Christmas seasons, predict that God will comfort his people and restore them to their own land. Usually, though not always, this is to be accomplished through a Jewish kingdom like that of David but more glorious. A Child is born, who will be called the Prince of Peace (Isa. 9:6-7). The descendant of Jesse will have wisdom and fear of the Lord, and will execute righteous judgment. Earth itself will be transformed so that even the animal world knows peace; "they shall not hurt nor destroy in all my holy mountain" (Isa. 11:1-9). The fortieth chapter of Isaiah says nothing about an ideal king. The God to whom the nations are as a drop from the bucket, who takes up the isles as a very little thing, will himself come with a strong hand, and his arm will rule for him. He who never wearies nor faints will renew the strength of his people. "They shall run, and not be weary; and they shall walk, and not faint." The gospel of Second Isaiah is that "thy God reigneth" (Isa. 52:7).

It therefore does not matter that the precise phrase "Kingdom of the Heavens" or "Reign of the Heavens" (*malkuth ha-shamayim*), the regular way in which the rabbis expressed the idea, is not found in any Old Testament book. The idea is in the passages above and in such phrases as "his Kingdom," "thy Kingdom," and the frequent references to God as King (e.g. Ps. 145:11-13; I Chron. 29:11).

This conviction, that God's royal power will surely be exercised, reappears throughout the rabbinic literature. What the rabbis taught can be summarized as follows: God is by right king of the universe, he always has been and always will be. But man instead of recognizing this sovereignty has frequently rebelled. God offered Israel dominion of the earth as his vicegerent, and Israel accepted it by promising to obey his Law. When Israel failed in its obedience, God permitted power to pass to other nations, and so most of the earth is in open rebellion against him. But in so far as men take "the yoke of the Kingdom" upon them by acknowledging God's sovereignty and doing his will, his Kingdom is made effective among men. In the age to come God's Kingdom will be "revealed," the truth of his sovereignty will be manifest, and everything that opposes it will be done away. The Jewish liturgy contains more than one prayer that the Kingdom will be revealed and established.

One can therefore translate the phrase either as "Kingdom," "Reign," or "Sovereignty of God." Sometimes it refers to God's royal power and prerogative, sometimes to the sphere in which it is exercised. This is true in the Old Testament, in the rabbinic writings, and also in the teaching of Jesus.

What Jesus proclaimed specifically was that the Kingdom of God was at hand (Mark 1:15, *ēngiken*, has drawn near). He also taught his disciples to pray for the Kingdom to come, and Matthew's form of the Lord's Prayer adds the explanatory phrase, "thy will be done, as in heaven, so on earth" (Matt. 6:10; cf. Luke 11:2). The prayer's first clause, "May thy name be sanctified," means almost the same thing. God's Name is sanctified—that is, it is recognized as holy and men praise and thank him—when his righteous, generous and loving will is done. These passages make luminously clear both the nature of God's Reign and the promise of its future coming.

The Kingdom comes as God's gift, and Jesus' followers need only rely on God's promise (Luke 12:32). Jesus in his own ministry of the Good News is sowing the seed which assures the advent of the Kingdom. Though some of the seed falls on a rocky ledge, or on the road or among thorns, the harvest will be out of all proportion to the sowing (Mark 4:1-9). What seems as small and insignificant as a mustardseed will become a great shrub in which the birds of the air build their nests (4:30-32). Probably few readers of this parable recognize a clear reminiscence of Daniel 4:1-18, in which Nebuchadnezzar's kingdom is compared to a tree reaching as high as the sky, in the boughs of which dwell the fowls of heaven. But this tree is cut down and the king of Babylon is driven from the haunts of men. It is an obvious contrast between the old, temporary kingdoms of this world and the new Reign of God. The parable of the leaven (Matt. 13:33=Luke 13:20-21) promises that the Kingdom will burst forth dramatically and irresistibly just as yeast working in a mass of dough causes it to grow and overflow its trough. What is hidden and unrecognized now will appear glorious and inescapable.

Yet the Kingdom is present now, or at least the first signs of its operation are visible. "If I by the finger of God cast out demons, then the Kingdom of God has overtaken you" (Luke 11:20; cf. Matt. 12:28). Another, somewhat obscure saying, draws a contrast between the era of the Law and Prophets, which was until the time of John, and the new time when the Kingdom of God is proclaimed (Matt. 11:12-13; Luke 16:16). Many prophets and kings (or righteous men) have wished in vain to see what is now open to the disciples' vision (Matt. 13:16-17=Luke 10:23-24). "The Kingdom of God is in your midst" (Luke 17:21)—or perhaps we should translate "within your reach," since the Greek word unfortunately is ambiguous.

The Kingdom will surely come, but this does not guarantee that everyone will share in its benefits. "Not everyone who calls me Lord, Lord shall enter into the Kingdom of the Heavens" (Matt. 7:21), but only those who do God's will. The Kingdom is open to the poor, who know their need, those who mourn for the world's sin, the meek, those who hunger and thirst for righteousness, the merciful, the single-minded, the peacemakers, the persecuted (Matt. 5:3-11)—in a word, sinners who respond to the Good News and accept it with open gratitude. To enter the Kingdom one must become like a little child, not bargaining but accepting a free gift (Mark 10:15; Matt. 18:3). This idea is not far from that of the Laborers in the Vineyard (Matt. 20:1-15), for in both instances what God gives immeasurably exceeds man's deserving.

He who accepts God's Reign is ready to give up anything else for it. A man discovers a treasure hidden in a field and out of joy he goes and sells everything he has to buy that field (Matt. 13:44). The illustration of the pearl of great price is still clearer: a man has found one pearl of matchless beauty and sells everything he has to possess it (13:45-46). He owns nothing else in the world, but he has the pearl! This is not sacrifice, as people ordinarily think of the word—it is the satisfaction of having what is most worth while, the achievement of heart's desire.

Students of Jesus' teaching in their preoccupation with the words "king" and "kingdom" may easily forget that they are, after all, metaphors. For the member of the Kingdom of God is not just a subject of the realm, he is also a child of God. The parable of the Prodigal Son is not essentially different from those of the Laborers in the Vineyard and the Great Supper. All refer to the same relationship. The term "Family of God" is just as appropriate as "Kingdom." The royal vocabulary emphasizes the point that, unlike human fathers, God is a father whose power and claim on man are absolute. The word "Father" reminds Jesus' hearers that God is not like other kings. Both ideas are complementary ways of describing God, whose power and love cannot be fully expressed, but only suggested by metaphors.

Therefore, to enter the Kingdom is essentially to recognize and accept and claim a relationship which God has always intended, though man has often broken it. It is not enough to call Jesus Lord, or give verbal assent to his teaching, or claim a personal acquaintance with him. All these must lead to the new relationship to God and a turning away from anything that hinders this relationship. One who follows this way may at first appear to pay a high price, but in fact he has become immensely wealthy. He is prince in a world kingdom, the son of his Father, secure in the love of the home.

"Kingdom of God," then, describes a family relationship and the making of God's will effective. When this is recognized, it becomes easier to deal with the question whether the Kingdom is present or future. As Millar Burrows has pointed out, the prayer "thy Kingdom come" shows where the emphasis lies. There can be no doubt that Jesus most often spoke of God's Reign as coming.

On the other hand, there are the few "present Kingdom" sayings, quoted above; that is, those which suggest the immediate presence of the Kingdom. Attempts to explain them have been manifold. Many have taken them to refer to the Christian Church—either as a definite, organized society or a spiritual kingdom which manifests itself in the existing churches. The strongest argument for this view is Jesus' teaching that one can enter the Kingdom, and enter it only under certain conditions. But there is no reason to think that he identified the Kingdom as a visible, distinct human society with a specific organization and constitution. Matthew's two sayings which mention the word "church" (16:17-19; 18:15-20) are open to question because they are unique in the gospels. They are contained in that gospel which is most concerned with the practical affairs of the organized church and in which Peter is the hero and typical disciple. The famous passage in chapter 16 looks like the utterance of a Christian prophet after the Resurrection. Peter's acknowledgment of Jesus as Messiah is the rock on which the Church is founded, and even the gates of death—the death of Jesus or his followers—will not prevail against the Church, or perhaps against the truth on which it is built. Even the parable of the dragnet (Matt. 13:47-48) says only that the preaching of the Kingdom now gathers all kinds of people; at the end of the age they will be sorted out. The Manual of Discipline gives a good example of a messianic movement organized as a visible church under divine sanction. The gospels are in the strongest possible contrast to this. If Jesus had planned a church with a definite constitution, it is strange that his directions have been so completely lost and that those sayings which are claimed as directions are so ambiguous.

In another passage Jesus promises that the Twelve will sit on thrones judging the twelve tribes of Israel (Luke 22:28-30=Matt. 19:28). This saying is not connected with a future earthly church but with the coming age and the Messianic Banquet, i.e. the Kingdom of God. However, according to Mark 10:40, even Jesus himself cannot give his disciples places of honor in the Kingdom; this is the sole prerogative of God. Thus every possible reference to the Church or its leaders is oriented to the final coming age. Burrows is right: the emphasis is on the words "thy Kingdom come."

Another popular theory about the "present Kingdom" sayings would interpret the Kingdom of God as existing only in the hearts and minds of converted individuals. The Kingdom of God thus becomes a network of ethical and spiritual relationships between man and God, and the emphasis tends to be put on the individual, his spiritual condition, and his personal relationship to God. The watchword of this school of thought is "The Kingdom of God is within you" (Luke 17:21) —a sentence that may be a mistranslation. Such a theory suggests part of the truth, but only part, because it ignores the supreme tension between present and future which is basic in the teaching of Jesus, and can easily ignore the social character of the Kingdom or Family of God.

These two ideas—that the Kingdom of God is a specific church or group of churches or that it exists in the hearts of men as a purely ideal and invisible reality—are both modernizations. They are attempts to understand Jesus' teaching from some perspective other than his own.

On the other hand, the so-called "eschatological" school of New Testament critics has waved the "present Kingdom" sayings aside too arbitrarily. These scholars have argued that the Kingdom is present only in anticipation, by way of a prophetic glimpse into the future. It is not really present at all; Jesus does no more than to say that the present gleams of light forecast the rising of the sun. This is to forget the Jewish teaching that man can take the yoke of the Kingdom of God upon himself, an idea which surely must lie in the background of Jesus' teaching.

It seems, therefore, that the Kingdom of God is not merely a future hope but is also in some real sense present in the world. Here we are thrown back to the Old Testament and Jewish ideas of the Kingdom.

The parables show that Jesus and his disciples are proclaiming the Kingdom of God and many people are actually accepting and entering it. They become members of what is both a Kingdom and a family. They are restored to their true relationship with their Father and with one another, the family life which God had always intended. In so far as this happens, the Kingdom of God is not something future and far-off but a concrete fact in this world. What is new is that the miracle now occurs on such a large scale and with such dramatic results. The blind receive their sight, the lame walk, lepers are cleansed and the deaf hear, the dead are raised and the poor hear the Good News (Matt. 11:4-5=Luke 7:22). The Law and the Prophets, even John the Baptist himself, belong to the old age; now is the age of the Kingdom of God (Matt. 11:12-13=Luke 16:16)! These present manifestations of the reality and activity of God's Reign prove to Jesus that the prayer will be answered and the Kingdom is "coming" in some more transcendent and universal way.

Whether the coming Kingdom might be established on the earth as human beings know it, or on an earth so changed that one should call it "heaven," it would mark a complete revolution in human affairs. Jesus' teaching was of course a judgment on all kingdoms of this world. It has often been asked, what kind of society did Jesus contemplate? Professor Frederick C. Grant has described Jesus' ministry as the last great agrarian revolt of antiquity, the demand that the world return to the justice, love and mutual responsibility of family and tribal life, in which men live as those who have one father and one sheikh.[1] Or one might describe Jesus' protest in sociological language. There are certain primary relationships of life, such as the family, which are permanent in nature and cannot be broken without deep hurt and distintegration of personality, and there are secondary, more fortuitous relationships that are often dissolved at will. Man becomes less than human when his connections are mostly secondary in nature; he is rootless, a member of a proletariat. As such, in modern society he is only an employe, a taxpayer, a voter, a conscript into the armed forces, a consumer; as such, like a part in an automobile, society regards him as replaceable and expendable. We do not know enough about ancient society to tell how many people were lonely and adrift in the first century. We do have evidence of massacres and the relative cheapness of human life. We know that in the empire magic, astrology and divination flourished, and that some of the new cults and philosophies

[1] F. C. Grant, *An Introduction to New Testament Thought* (New York, 1950), pp. 303-7.

offered individuals a meaning in life and a sense of brotherhood. One can readily believe that Jesus sensed the break-
down of human life which took place as royal or imperial
power reached more deeply into society. Without being
a social theorist like some of the Greek philosophers, he
knew the cure for the malady: men must and can live in
a more intensely personal and outreaching way and treat
even their enemies as members of God's family like themselves.

But this is not a "program" for action. Matters are not
solved by reorganizing society on a sheikhly basis, for, as
the Old Testament testifies, this simpler and more personal organization was infected by evil. The Kingdom
which Jesus foresaw was patriarchal only in the sense of
the patriarchal *ideal*; it was a family in which order, freedom and love were the rule. It stood, and it still stands,
as a warning that any social order will break down in
which man is less than a prince and a child of God, but
it is not a pattern that can be expressed in a constitution
and statutes. One cannot even call Jesus a religious anar-
chist, for he had no plan for the disappearance of government.

When Jesus speaks of the Kingdom of God it is not
to say what man should do but *what God is doing*. Through
the proclamation of the Good News, God reaches out to
man and gathers him into his Kingdom. The individual
finds that the meaning of his life is changed. His relationships—even in his natural family—take on a new perspective. He feels a greater responsibility than before as a
member of his human family and the Jewish Commonwealth, and he has also become part of a colony of heaven.
The earliest Christians probably did not think of themselves
as a sect in Judaism, or even as a party. They were simply

bearers of a message which would transform the world. As soon as they perceived the universal implications of their message, a universal church became inevitable. On the one hand, the Jewish nation generally rejected their proclamation so that they were driven to form a separate group. On the other hand, the gospel itself constituted them as a unity. They acted and thought together because, as the Book of Acts says, "the multitude of believers was of one heart and one life" (Acts 4:32)—not perfectly and ideally, but actually to an unusually high degree. Intimately connected with the gospel were two ritual acts which Jesus taught his fellowers—the Lord's Prayer and the common meal which was itself a foretaste of the coming Kingdom—and these reinforced the unity. Thus, while Jesus made no plans and gave no directions for a church distinct from Judaism, he took certain actions which must inevitably have one of two results. Either the Jewish nation had to accept his message and become its bearer to mankind, or his disciples had to go their own way, at whatever cost, and seek out the future heirs of the Kingdom wherever they might be found.

Jesus does not describe the political and social pattern which the Kingdom of God will take when finally it appears, nor does he indicate the process by which it comes. He contents himself with parables and metaphors which express its glory and joy, and which call men into it and bid them prepare for it. The continued preaching of the Good News is certainly a preparation for the Kingdom. It may be true that the extension of Christianity as an organized religion, and the achievement of a more just and peaceful world order, are instruments which God will eventually use in the establishment of his Kingdom. Jesus' concern for justice and mercy is a proof that he would commend a better social order, and a better church. But he does not address himself to any of these issues. His concern is to call individuals and the groups of his followers to immediate obedience. Whatever society may do, whatever they can do about society, they must get their own hearts and minds straight, and think and behave as children of God. However necessary and right political action may be, conversion must start with the individual and the groups with which he is most intimately and deeply associated. The manner of the Kingdom's coming is God's business; man's task is simply to believe, obey and rejoice.

The apocalypses, both Jewish and Christian, offered indications of the time when the end should come. Did Jesus make such predictions? The testimony of the gospel tradition is not entirely consistent. According to Mark 13, the last days begin with preliminary troubles—wars, earthquakes, famines and persecutions. The gospel must be preached to all nations before the end can come. Then, apparently, comes the abomination that makes desolate and a more serious persecution than any that have gone before. Finally sun, moon and stars fail, and people see the Son of Man coming in the clouds to gather the elect. At the end of the chapter it is said that all this will occur before the present generation passes away, though even the Son does not know the exact day and hour. Matthew's parallel passage (chap. 24) adds several details from other sources. The other parallel, chapter 21 of Luke, changes the prophecy of the abomination of desolation into a prediction that Jerusalem will be destroyed. As a result, Luke places the end of the age in "this generation" but some time after the Jewish War. Matthew and Luke are clearly composite and a careful reading of Mark 13 suggests that it, too, is a compilation of traditional materials not all of which consist in words of Jesus.

Other parables and sayings of Jesus give a teaching very different from that of Mark 13. "This generation is a wicked generation; it seeks a sign, and no sign will be given it except the sign of Jonah. For as Jonah was a sign to the Ninevites"—and this sign was the message of repentance—"so will the Son of Man be to this generation" (Luke 11:30). Here the Son of Man is not the figure who comes on the clouds of heaven, but simply Jesus himself as he carries on his regular ministry; God himself will give them no other sign.

In another place, Luke 17:20-37, "Son of Man" denotes the coming Judge, but the emphasis is on the sudden and unexpected judgment when he is revealed. Jesus' discourse begins with the words, "The Kingdom of God does not come with observation" (17:20)—there is no astronomical way of figuring the time of its coming. The essential teaching of the passage is that, as in ancient days, people will be unprepared for the cataclysm. Some will be rescued and others left to destruction; in other words, it will be an individual judgment.

Still other sayings of Jesus threaten a judgment but teach that the signs of it—like the sign of Jonah—are just such as any man should be able to discern without the help of special revelation. If Palestinians can predict a rain or a hot wind, they should surely know the signs of the time (Luke 12:54-56). Even disasters, such as the slaughter of the Galileans and the fall of the tower of Siloam are no indication of God's vengeance on those particular individuals, they are only examples of a warning to all (Luke 13:1-5). Certainly Jesus saw that the nation, with its wickedness and violence, was hastening to a catastrophe, but there is nothing in these sayings to suggest that he made a definite prediction or connected the coming war with the end of the world.

His almost contemptuous rejection of signs comes out in the parable of the rich man and Lazarus. To seek for certainty about the after-life is a desire even more natural than the yearning for exact information about the end of the world. Is there a judgment? Do the decisions of this life make a difference in the next? The rich man asks that he be sent back to his kindred so that he may warn them before it is too late. "They have Moses and the prophets," says Abraham; "let them listen to them." "Oh, no, Father Abraham, but if someone went to them from the dead they would repent." "If they do not listen to Moses and the prophets, they will not be persuaded even if one were to rise from the dead" (Luke 16:19-31).

These sayings have the mark of Jesus' individuality, and all of them have much the same point. They must be taken as decisive. In the Old Testament God had already set before man the two ways, of life and of death. Sufficient warning had been given. It was necessary for Jesus only to expose the essential meaning of the old revelation—to make clear the heart of the Law as distinct from specific enactments—and to proclaim the Good News of forgiveness and power. Special revelations dealing with the world's future were beside the point and distracted man from his immediate duty.

It is certainly true that Jesus saw his world as standing at the edge both of destruction and the Kingdom of God. The apocalyptic temper of Palestine in the first century led both Jews and Christians to look on thir own generation as the decisive moment in world history. And, whatever fantastic forms the future hope may have taken here and there, the mood of this century forced religious man to look at the ultimates. As someone has said, for a whole generation the attention of man was turned away from lesser interests toward the essential issues of life—faith and unfaith, good and evil, life and death. Perhaps the man of faith always looks at life with something of this perspective, for each generation faces the perils and glorious opportunities of man's brief life. As for Jesus himself, we cannot prove from our sources either that he believed in the near end of the world or that he did not. The very ambiguity of the gospels, plus his rejection of miraculous signs, makes it very probable that he gave no answer to the question. There can be no doubt, however, that he gave a clear teaching directed toward the mingled hope and fear of his own generation. He said, in effect: whatever the exact plan of God may be, now is the time for decision; you will never have another time and you must act before it is too late; the Kingdom of God is open to you, accept it and enter it as a child of God.

Jesus took this position because he believed so profoundly in God and his kingship. God occupied the whole of his religious horizon. To all the first-century Jews who had programs of deliverance for the people of Israel— Pharisaism, national revolution, even the apocalyptic eschatology which counts fondly on times and seasons— he said the same word: "Your thoughts are not the thoughts of God but the thoughts of men" (Mark 8:33). He shared the lot of his Palestinian brothers; he sympathized deeply with them in the sense that he knew and understood their miseries and aspirations. But his perspective was not Galilean or national. It was determined in the strictest sense by his citizenship in the Kingdom of God,

CHAPTER IX

THE MISSION OF JESUS

JESUS' work led him at last to his death. Behind this there is a mystery, for although his fearless and independent teaching certainly aroused opposition, it is hard to see how the teaching alone could explain the Crucifixion. He was executed by the Roman authorities, if not for the alleged crime of high treason, then at least as a possibly seditious person who endangered the peace. This means that someone was bitterly enough opposed to him to bring the accusation; and that the case had just enough plausibility so that Pilate would not, or could not, acquit him. Does this mean that Jesus claimed to be Messiah, and that this title was then understood as "King of the Jews"? Is there something in the nature of Jesus' vocation that explains both the teacher of Galilee and the Crucified One of Jerusalem?

Our Lord's own conception of his work has been endlessly investigated and no one can present a solution that will command universal acceptance. We can do no more than to present an hypothesis covering as many of the facts as possible.

The evangelists look back on the events from the vantage point of Christian faith, and it is on them that we depend for our information. They presume that he must have been fully conscious of his position as Messiah and Son of God. Christ as portrayed in the Gospel of John seems to be omniscient. He knows that he has come out from the Father, and with calm joy he looks forward to the time when he shall return to the heavenly sphere. For the benefit of his hearers he prays aloud, but within himself he has no need for verbal prayer, for his communion with the Father is constant and unbroken. He asserts his claim to be Son of God—or rather reminds his hearers that Moses and the prophets have already borne testimony to him—and this is not because he seeks glory for himself but for the sake of the salvation of mankind.

No such complete theology is found in the other gospels, but the synoptics contain many sayings and stories that point in the same direction, and the editorial changes which Matthew and Luke make in their earlier sources indicate that the approach of these evangelists is not essentially different from that of John. Luke occasionally uses the phrase "my father" (2:49; 22:29) but it is more frequently found in Matthew, usually in the form "my father who is in the heavens" (7:21; 10:32-33; 11:25-27; 15:13; 16:17; 18:10, 19; 20:23). One passage, indeed, approaches the Johannine position (Matt. 11:25-30, partly paralleled in Luke 10:21-22). Here Jesus offers a solemn thanksgiving to his Father that he has hidden the revelation from the wise and prudent and revealed it to babes. No one knows the Son except the Father, and no one can know the Father except through the Son. The section concludes with an appeal to humanity to come to the Son, to accept his yoke, which is light, and so find true rest and refreshment.

Mark, the author of our earliest gospel, teaches from the beginning of his book to the end that Jesus is Son of God. The demons perceive this truth long before it is revealed to the disciples. In the parable of the Wicked Husbandmen (12:1-12) Jesus seems to imply that he himself is God's Son who was cast out of the vineyard and put to death. The stories of the Baptism and the Trans-figuration witness to the divine sonship.

Part of the Son's vocation, according to Mark, was to be the Messiah expected by the Jewish people, who would restore the ancient glories of David's kingdom. But, as Mark portrays this, the conception of Messiah as warrior and king is partly negated and completely transformed. The Messiah has taken on the title and characteristics of the Son of Man, the heavenly judge of the Book of Enoch, who comes on the clouds at the end of the world. Yet before he can be fully revealed he must suffer and die, like the Servant of the Lord in Second Isaiah, who was wounded for our transgressions and by whose stripes we are healed. At Caesarea Philippi, Peter recognizes Jesus as Messiah and in turn Jesus identifies himself as Son of Man. Finally, before the high priest, Jesus acknowledges his dual rôle.

Lying behind Matthew and Luke is a body of sayings and anecdotes which most scholars call Q and which is thought to come from a written document. Here again, in the Temptation story (Matt. 4:1-11=Luke 4:1-13) Jesus is Son of God. But he most often speaks of himself as Son of Man. The passages employing the title are sharply divided. In about half of them the Son of Man is the future judge, as in Mark, but Jesus does not clearly iden-tify himself with that figure. In the other half, "Son of Man" simply means "I, Jesus," and nothing is said of his work at the end of the age.

A group of sayings, scattered here and there through the gospels, is marked by the phrase "I have come." For ex-ample, Jesus has not come to destroy but to fulfil the Law (Matt. 5:17), not to bring peace but a sword (Matt.

10:34=Luke 12:51), not to call the righteous but sinners (Mark 2:17).

All of the above evidence is impressive. It suggests that Jesus consciously accepted a special vocation to Israel as something far more than a teacher or even as prophet. If it were established that he openly acknowledged his Messiahship, and that this was generally known, historians would find it easier to explain why the Crucifixion took place. In that case, even if he came to Jerusalem meek and lowly, riding on an ass, everyone else in the city would have taken him for what we call a man on horseback. It belonged to the definition of Messiah that his dominion should be from the one sea to the other, and from the River Euphrates to the world's end; all kings should fall down before him, his enemies should lick the dust. It was God's Kingdom, to be sure, but administered through the Jewish nation, with an earthly monarch at its head.

The earliest modern life of Christ, that of Reimarus, actually put forth the hypothesis that Jesus claimed kingship and was in some sense a revolutionist; in our own generation Robert Eisler has revived Reimarus' notion.[1] But when the gospels are investigated more fully, not only is this theory destroyed but there is a serious question whether Jesus gave much specific teaching about his vocation.

One may begin with Matthew's rewriting of Mark. Peter's confession at Caesarea Philippi, according to Mark, is answered with a command to be silent and an explanation that the Son of Man must suffer. When Peter protests, Jesus rebukes him with the words, "Get behind me [get

---

[1] Hermann Samuel Reimarus, *Von dem Zwecke Jesu und seiner Jünger* (Brunswick, 1778); R. Eisler, *The Messiah Jesus* (New York, 1931).

out of my sight?], Satan, for you are not thinking the thoughts of God but of man" (Mark 8:27-33). Matthew inserts a different saying after Peter's word of faith: "Blessed are you, Simon, son of Jonah, because flesh and blood has not revealed it to you, but my Father who is in the heavens" (Matt. 16:17). There are other examples in Matthew of the evangelist's desire to show that Jesus accepted the title Messiah, for example 23:10.

The evangelists have included such sayings as these, not out of any conscious desire to distort the picture, but because they write from the perspective of the Christian Church. A number of the passages in which Jesus speaks of his vocation look like the utterances of early Christian prophets. In the first and second centuries preaching was not merely teaching and exposition of scripture; often it was prophecy. The prophet sometimes stepped out of his own personality and spoke on behalf of the risen Christ. Ignatius, bishop of Antioch, says, "When I was among you, I cried out, I spoke with a great voice, with the voice of God" (Ign. Philad. 7:1). In the letters to the seven churches in the Book of Revelation (Rev. 1:17–3:22) there is a good example of what such a voice might say. It is worth while to read the section carefully, noting particularly the phrase "I am" (1:17) which is also characteristic of the Fourth Gospel, and to compare it with the conclusion of a second-century sermon preached at Easter by Melito, bishop of Sardis:

> "I," he says, "am the Christ, I am he who destroyed death and triumphed over the enemy and trod down Hades and bound the Strong Man and brought man to haven in the heights of the heavens; I," he says, "am Christ . . . For I am your forgiveness, I the Pass-over of salvation, the lamb slain for you, I am your

ransom, I am your light, I am your saviour, I am your resurrection, I am your king. . . ."[2]

In the light of early Christian practice, it would not be strange if such passages as Matt. 11:25-30; 5:17-19; 16:17-19; 18:18-20; 23:8-10, 34-36 (=Luke 11:49-51) were spoken by prophets some time after the Crucifixion. Early Christians probably saw no essential difference between these and historical words of Jesus that had been handed down; both were taken up into the gospel tradition.

More important is the positive evidence that Jesus was reluctant to define his own relationship to God or to accept the titles which were offered him. The confession of Peter at Caesarea Philippi is a case in point. Later on in the Gospel of Mark, blind Bartimaeus addresses Jesus as Son of David (10:48), a title that obviously means Messiah. Once more, at the triumphal entry, the crowd shouts "Blessed is the coming kingdom of our father David" (11:10). Evidently there were many who regarded Jesus as the Davidic Messiah, but according to Mark, Jesus did nothing to encourage this identification, at least not until the hearing before the high priest (14:61-62). This is not surprising, if one remembers that Messiah meant one thing and one thing only to Palestinian Jews.

Evidence for the title Son of Man also illustrates the reticence of Jesus. The gospels never use the phrase except in words of the Lord, and it is therefore very likely that he often employed it to refer to himself. But it is a very ambiguous term, since it can mean "human being" or perhaps "prophet" (as in Ezekiel) as well as "heavenly judge." And it is significant that sometimes Jesus uses it

---

[2] Campbell Bonner, ed., *The Homily on the Passion by Melito Bishop of Sardis,* "Studies and Documents, XII" (London, 1940), p. 180.

in such a way that his hearers could not have told whether he or someone else was the Son of Man.

Another story tells of John the Baptist sending messengers to Jesus with the question "Are you he who is coming, or should we look for another?" There is no direct answer, only the command to "go and report to John the things that you hear and see" (Matt. 11:2-6=Luke 7:18-23). When challenged by members of the Sanhedrin in Jerusalem to tell by what authority he acts, Jesus again refuses to give an answer (Mark 11:27-36). This story implies that his authority, like that of John the Baptist, is directly from God.

On two occasions he corrects those who try to praise him. The rich man addresses him as "Good teacher," and receives the answer, "Why do you call me good? There is only one who is good; that is, God" (Mark 10:17-18). An enthusiastic woman exclaims—so we may paraphrase it— "How happy is your mother to have a son like you!" but Jesus replies, "No, rather, happy are those who hear the Word of God and keep it" (Luke 11:28). One point at least is clear. Jesus wishes to direct attention away from his own goodness, his own activities, even his work as teacher, toward God's word, God's mighty acts, and God's absolute goodness.

We are not dependent on the synoptic gospels alone. The Apostle Paul more than once emphasizes the humility and creatureliness of his Lord. When he became man, he renounced his divine prerogatives, took the nature of a slave, and carried his obedience to the point of dying on the Cross (Phil. 2:5-11). God's son was born of a woman, born under law (Gal. 4:4). He was crucified through weakness, though he lives through the power of God (II Cor. 13:4). Perhaps Paul had the example of Jesus in mind when he said that love "seeks not its own" (I Cor. 13:5). Even the Fourth Evangelist, who emphasizes Jesus' divine nature to an extreme degree, recalls that he did not seek glory for himself (John 7:16-18; 8:50-54). All this evidence surely comes from the memories of early Christians.

Here we are faced with contradictions in the gospel tradition; and it is worth remembering that there are a a number of discrepancies, real or apparent, in what is reported as Jesus' teaching. For example, one of the mission discourses bids the disciples be shod with sandals (Mark 6:9) while another forbids footwear (Luke 10:4). A passage in the Sermon on the Mount tells how the disciples ought to fast (Matt. 6:16-18) while elsewhere fasting is considered inappropriate—this present time is like a wedding party (Mark 2:19)! Twice the disciples are given definite authority to cast out demons (Mark 3:15; 6:7) but elsewhere they discover to their joyful surpise that they have the power (Luke 10:17). A few passages, found only in Matthew, range Jesus unequivocally on the side of the Law and the Pharisaic teaching (Matt. 5:17-20; 23:2-3) but elsewhere in the gospels (particularly Matt. 5:33-37; Mark 7:1-23 and most of Luke 11:37–12:1) Jesus is highly independent of the Pharisees and even the written Law.

If we are to ask what Jesus actually taught about himself and his own work, it is not sufficient to marshal passages on one side or the other, but we must find some other way through the gospel material. The first thing to realize is that concentration on such words as "Messiah," "Son of Man," and "Son of God" may lead one astray. None of these terms, except perhaps Messiah, has a precise denotation; its meaning depends on who uses it and the context in which it is used. Even "Messiah" suggested one thing to a non-Christian Jew and something quite different to the evangelists and St. Paul. It may be more important to find out what attitude Jesus took toward his own work and what kind of authority he exercised over his disciples, than to ask what title he accepted or rejected.

Beyond any doubt, Jesus was strong and aggressive as a teacher. He evoked either allegiance or hostility. In only one place—his native village—are we told that people were lukewarm. According to Mark, his neighbors regarded him as only a countryman and refused to take him seriously (Mark 6:1-6). His bitter prophetic words on Chorazin, Bethsaida and Capernaum suggest that in this important scene of activity he had been decisively rejected (Matt. 11:21-24=Luke 10:13-15). Herod Antipas, on hearing of his activity, thought that he must be a prophet like John the Baptist—it was as if John had risen from the dead (Mark 6:14). Enemies accused him of casting out demons by means of Beelzebul (Matt. 12:24=Luke 11:15). Others stigmatized him as a glutton and a wine-soak, a friend of tax-collectors and sinners (Matt. 11:19=Luke 7:34).

The testimony of his friends tallies with that of his enemies in one important respect. Mark speaks frequently —even though allowances should be made for the evangelist's repetitive style—of astonishment at his teachings and healings, and the awe which he evoked. Authority, inner power, was Jesus' outstanding quality. Unlike the scribes, who cited previous tradition and scriptural passages, he taught with authority (Mark 1:22). In the same way he commanded the unclean spirits (1:27). His disciples, as they followed him to Jerusalem, were afraid (10:32).

When Jesus deals with adverse criticism he speaks

with complete certainty. At the same time he often appeals
to reason or to the Old Testament. In two cases of
healing on the Sabbath, he argues that if one can show
mercy to animals one can surely help human beings (Luke
13:16; 14:5). His defense of plucking grain on the Sabbath is based partly on scripture and partly on the principle
that "Man (or the Son of Man) is master of the Sabbath"
(Mark 2:23-28). More than once, when dealing with carp-
ing opponents, he uses the method of a debater. He points
out that he and John the Baptist are criticized for opposite
things—the criticisms cancel one another out (Matt.
11:16-19=Luke 7:31-35). When charged with using
demonic power to cast out demons, he argues that the
power must come either from Beelzebul or from God. If
it is from the former, then the charge of sorcery can lie
with equal justice on the "sons" of the Pharisees. Furthermore, the accusation is absurd: Satan is not so stupid as to
work against his own purposes. But if the power is from
God it is a sure sign of the presence of the Kingdom (Matt.
12:25-28=Luke 11:17-20). Behind this is the calm certainty that Jesus, and all others who rescue humanity, are
working on the side of God and his Kingdom.

Sometimes, as in the instance just cited, Jesus attacks
directly. To ascribe to Satan the best deed in the world—
the healing of mental illness—is to blaspheme the Holy
Spirit (Mark 3:28-30 and parallels). Equally trenchant
is his defense of his ministry to sinners and outcasts. In
at least three parables, the Great Supper, the Laborers
in the Vineyard, and the Prodigal Son, his point is the
same: the offer of good news and healing to these groups
is the activity of God, it is God's invitation, and to call
it in question is to question God's rightness and to fight
against him. This is the activity of a prophet, though of

one who appeals more often than the Old Testament prophets to the reason and commonsense of his fellows.

His lawgiving is of the same prophetic character. Jesus declares with authority the basis on which people will be blessed and accepted by God. Their righteousness must exceed that of the scribes and Pharisees. They must become like little children. It is the poor, those who hunger and mourn, the peacemakers, the meek, who stand a better chance of entering the Kingdom than the rich or the conventionally religious. They must be ready to cut off hand or foot, or to lose an eye—in other words, to sacrifice what seems most dear—rather than lose the present chance of salvation. His formula "You have heard that it was said to the ancients . . . but I say to you" implies complete authority to interpret and reform the written Law.

Yet he shows no interest in replacing an old code with a new one. He gives a few examples that modify or abolish ceremonial law, and a few principles by which the moral demand is intensified. Most of his other teaching is in the form of parables and examples which suggest the urgency of the time and the joy of the Kingdom of God. In all this he teaches with authority, and not as the scribes.

The parables of the Kingdom never say in so many words that he is the bringer of the Kingdom or its unique harbinger. But they seem to suggest at every point that he stands on God's side and is the agent by whom the message comes to men. He is inevitably involved in the sowing of the seed, the invitation to come to dinner, and the offer of work in the vineyard. Indeed his own activity is portrayed here; his ministry acts out the pictures given in the parables.

As the herald of the Kingdom he exercises leadership over his followers. "Follow me and I will make you into fishers of men" (Mark 1:15). He assumes that at his command they will leave everything and follow him. Followers must be ready to share the lot of Jesus, who has nowhere to lay his head (Matt. 8:20=Luke 9:58). With perhaps deliberate hyperbole, he says that they must not even delay long enough to bury their dead (Matt. 8:22= Luke 9:60). Hostility and even family strife will be the experience of his disciples (Luke 10:2; Matt. 10:34-39= Luke 12:51-53; 14:26-27). It is not necessary for him to give signs, either to prove the authority or the truth of his teaching; in fact he often disavows any intention to offer proof (Luke 17:22-37; 11:29; cf. Mark 8:11-12; Luke 16:19-31). There can be no credentials for prophets except their fruits (Matt. 7:15). When he is rejected he does not retaliate (Matt. 5:38-41; Luke 9:51-56) but he goes elsewhere, where there is some prospect of being heard. Although he states principles of righteousness, and demands positive performance and not mere profession, he seems to disavow that kind of pastoral leadership which is always inspecting and reforming (Matt. 7:1-5=Luke 6: 37-38, 41-42).

Throughout the gospel materials we have the picture of one who is not interested in authority for himself and who exercises it only because it is laid on him by God. He claims obedience not to himself but to God, and he claims obedience because he is obedient. He expects his disciples to behave like himself and to parallel his own ministry. They are told that the one who is first must be last, and the servant and slave of all (Mark 9:35; 10:43-44); this precisely defines his own position. One must remember this to understand the apostolic principle which appears in several forms: "He who listens to you listens to me, and he who rejects you rejects me; but he who rejects me rejects him who sent me" (Matt. 10:16; cf. Matt. 10:40; John 12:44-45; 13:20). No disciple can be above his teacher; the most that can be said is that he is like his teacher (Matt. 10:24=Luke 6:40). The authority which Jesus possesses, and which he gives his disciples, is not a full and undefined power; it is the authority to put before men the promises and demands of God and to call them to direct allegiance to God. This leadership carries with it the responsibility to serve one's brothers with humility; it is the absolute antithesis of what the world calls authority.

As a religious teacher, Jesus is unique. He has some of the traits of rabbi and wise man, frequently using folk wisdom and commonsense maxims to point a truth. A strong element of oriental humor, and a keen sense of the ludicrous, mark many of his sayings; and when he is humorous or ironic he is, of course, most deeply serious. His parables are illuminated with unforgettable poetic imagery, but in form they resemble rabbinic stories more than the oracles of the Old Testament prophets. He combines the word and activity of the prophet with that of the teacher and wise man; he is the synthesis of all three.

But he goes far beyond the prophets, for he consciously stands at the beginning of a new age. Jesus never claims to be going back to the tried and tested ways of the desert, the era of the Exodus, or the time of David and the prophets. He looks to the future and the present. Without denying that most of the tradition is good and true, he has a word so clear and so compelling that he does not even have to identify it as a word of God. It even takes precedence of the written word of the Bible. Jesus simply sees and speaks; and he seems often to assume that this truth is equally obvious to any right-minded man. In many ways he tries to show his hearers that a new era has come. Something greater than Jonah is here. The old wineskins are ruined; the gospel may be dangerous to what is old and once was useful, but nothing can stand in its way. The rabbis, like Paul, employ the metaphor of yeast to denote evil influence. Jesus, by a reversal of language, uses it to describe the Kingdom.

When he says that some of the heirs of the Kingdom have rejected it and others have taken their place, he claims, by implication, a sure and infallible insight into God's way of ruling his commonwealth. Boldly, unconditionally, he offers forgiveness of sins on behalf of God.

We conclude that the vocation of Jesus was unique and cannot be summed up in any of the titles used to describe it. He was apparently reluctant to be called Messiah. On occasion he described himself as prophet and perhaps Son of Man. But, like Messiah, he stood at the threshold of a new age. His work was principally to announce the new order but he also saw manifestations of its coming. In this sense he was also the bringer of the Kingdom of God. Despite his genuine humility, he was a leader who claimed unquestioning allegiance. He evoked loyalty from his followers, as though he were more than Messiah and more than prophet. His confident interpretation of the will of God, his close relationship to God, suggest that Mark's title Son of God is appropriate.

Opposition arose—the gospels from start to finish emphasize this—but Jesus also gained a large following. As Grant points out, Tacitus thinks of his ministry as a mass movement: "this pernicious superstition, checked for the moment, broke out again."[3] When all due allowances are

---

[3] F. C. Grant, *The Gospel of the Kingdom* (New York, 1940), pp. 4-6.

made for exaggeration of numbers, the fact remains that the gospels speak of the feeding of four or five thousand persons at the edge of the Sea of Galilee; Acts mentions a meeting of 120 brethren just after the Ascension (Acts 1:15) and the baptism of about three thousand (2:41); and Paul declares that on one occasion five hundred Christians, most of whom were still alive when he wrote, saw the risen Lord (I Cor. 15:6). Some of these adherents were more closely attached to Jesus than others, and they must have differed widely in their understanding of his message. No doubt many of them regarded him as Messiah and were eager to have him as their king. This would be sufficient to explain why the authorities feared Jesus. If we may trust Josephus' account, John the Baptist was put to death because he had too great a following.

But Jesus, at least in his Galilean ministry, never defined his mission and person. His authority spoke for itself. And it is on this inherent authority, rather than on any titles that he or others may have used to describe his vocation, that the Christian can most surely base his faith in Jesus as the incarnate Son of God. We do not know, we never can know, just why he said so little about himself. It is one of the stumbling-blocks of the synoptic gospels that he is so seldom represented as revealing his own place in the scheme of things. And yet for the Fourth Evangelist it is one of the glories of Jesus that he did not seek glory for himself.

We may be permitted to think that his silence is to be explained by his absolute allegiance to the Father God. He was simply not interested in that question which must be of paramount importance to all Christians, as it was to to his Galilean followers. The reason was that God's will took up his whole attention. It is this concentration upon

· CHAPTER X ·

JESUS IN JERUSALEM

THE last visit of Jesus to Jerusalem resulted in his death. The gospels say that he foresaw this, and there is evidence that he intended this visit to have a decisive result. But, apart from the purpose to preach and his readiness to die, the object of the visit is never clearly defined. Why did Jesus go to Jerusalem?

The evangelists explain that he went there to die. Mark includes in his gospel three predictions in which Jesus warns the disciples of his impending suffering, rejection and death (Mark 8:31; 9:31; 10:32-34). These impart a particular tone of solemnity to the gospel. Luke adds a pair of sayings which he thinks of as spoken in or near Galilee: "It is out of the question for a prophet to perish outside of Jerusalem. Jerusalem, Jerusalem, who dost kill the prophets and dost stone those who are sent to her, how many times I have wished to gather thy children as a hen gathers her brood under her wings, and thou wouldest not" (Luke 13:33-34).

All the evangelists see the last journey in the light of their conviction that the death of Jesus brought salvation to mankind. As believing Christians, we may accept this faith, and as historians we may agree that Jesus was ready to die rather than give up his mission. But his purpose was not merely to die. The gospel tradition remembers that Jesus thought his purpose might possibly be accomplished without his death. We are told that in the garden of Gethsemane he prayed, "Father, all things are possible for thee; take this cup away from me; yet not what I will but what thou wilt" (Mark 14:36). The prophetic figure of the lamb led to the slaughter does not adequately portray Jesus' attitude. As Alan Paton has said, he did not go up to Jerusalem to die; he went up to obey.

It was in Jerusalem that a battle had to be joined and a decision made. Presumably, Jesus went to the city to make a final appeal to the nation, solemnly gathered for a festival, to accept or reject his message of the Kingdom of God. It is curious that in the record of his teaching in Jerusalem the phrase "Kingdom of God" is not used. But many things in the tradition suggest that kingship is the issue. Who possesses authority over the nation? Who is the rightful king of Israel?

Jerusalem was the religious capital of Palestine—and, for Jews, it was the center of the world. Not the political capital at the moment, for Pilate's regular headquarters were in Caesarea. The principal importance of the city has always been religious. It has no adequate water supply of its own and no economic function save as a pilgrimage center. It is not even of supreme strategic importance, for conquerors of the Near East can by-pass it and seal it off until they are ready to take it. Its value is that it is the place where Araunah the Jebusite had a threshing-floor which became the place of God's glory, the city of David and Solomon and the kings, and later, the city of Jesus' crucifixion and resurrection and of Mohammed's ascension into heaven. It is important because people love it; and no city, not even Rome, has been more the land of heart's desire. "If I forget thee, O Jerusalem, let my right hand forget its cunning!" (Ps. 137:5).

According to Mark, Jesus came from Jericho to Jerusalem. On the way out of Jericho, the blind Bartimaeus hailed him as Messiah son of David. The road led past Bethany and Bethphage. As they rounded the Mount of Olives, a magnificent view awaited them; not the Turkish-built city with domed houses so well known today, but a city with new buildings, walls and towers constructed in the best Hellenistic fashion that Herod's architects could contrive. Across the deep ravine of the Kidron was the Temple area, its south end rising at a dizzy height above the vale of Hinnom, decked out with gates and colonnades and fair paved open spaces where the Jew, like today's pious Moslem, could converse, read, meditate, drink water and take naps; and at the west end of the Holy Place, beyond the great altar, the Holy of Holies building rose sharply into the air, its east face covered with beaten gold to catch and reflect the rays of the rising sun with terrible splendor. As in the Haram at Hebron, Herod had laid the foundations of the Temple area with huge stones, many of them still in place, beautifully dressed and fitted. Small wonder that the disciples of Jesus exclaimed, "Teacher, see! what stones and what buildings!" (Mark 13:1).

This magnificent architectural complex, whose construction kept on for another generation, did not bring the peace, stability and happiness for which its builders might have hoped. Strict rabbis had incited a riot when Herod the Great set the Roman eagle over its portal. To the northwest, overlooking the enclosure, was the fortress of the Antonia, where Roman soldiers were always on guard.

The city proper stretched west to about the line of the present wall, dominated by Herod's three great towers named Mariamne, Hippicus and Phasael. One of these still survives in rebuilt form at the Jaffa Gate as the so-called Tower of David. The city was laid out in Hellenistic fashion with one main east-west street and a north-south street crossing it at right angles, while smaller streets branched off from them. Robinson's Arch may have been the support of an elevated east-west thoroughfare which crossed the Tyropoeon valley and led to the Temple enclosure. In the center of the town was a market place and south of the city Herod had erected a theatre and a hippodrome. The old city of David, Ophel, may have been to the south of the Temple, where the vegetable gardens of Siloam are today. In these crowded slums the Pharisees had their greatest following, and perhaps their strict rules of purity kept houses and streets more clean and decent than one would expect in an ancient Near Eastern city.

The appearance of Jerusalem was Hellenistic, save as the orient here and there must have imparted a subtly different flavor. Greek was freely spoken, as well as Aramaic; scholars wrote and probably spoke Hebrew; and most people dressed in the Greek chiton and himation, yet the Jew had also his ceremonial tassels and phylacteries. The city was cosmopolitan. Largely populated by Palestinian Jews, there were visitors and residents from every nation where Jewish people had settled; the Book of Acts in its account of Pentecost speaks of Parthians and Medes and Elamites, inhabitants of Cappadocia, Pontus, Asia, Phrygia and Pamphylia, Egypt and Cyrenaica, Romans, Cretans and Arabians (Acts 2:9-11). An inscription in Greek tells us that Theodotus, son of Vettenos, built a synagogue in the city. Other archaeological discoveries from the centuries before and after Christ show that Egyptian, Greek and oriental art all met in Palestine. Pagans from Syria and Egypt must often have come to Jerusalem, as well as Roman soldiers and officials, and tribesmen must sometimes have come in from the desert.

Jerusalem has seldom known long periods of peace, save under the Byzantine empire, the Arabs and the Turks. These periods are marked off by bloody invasions, and the Arab rule was interrupted by the Crusades, which the Near East has never forgotten. The Hebrew monarchy was ridden with internal strife and foreign war; the brief period of independence under the Maccabees and the quasi-independence of Herod's dynasty were times of continual turmoil. Tension and alien domination have been the lot of Jerusalem.

It is always dangerous to attempt a reconstruction of ancient history by modern analogies. But anyone who was in Jerusalem at the time of the Arab uprising in 1936 or the Jewish terrorism eleven years later is apt to ask himself whether the emotional tone of Jerusalem under British mandate was not like that of the Roman city in the time of Jesus. In both cases, a world power from the west tried to maintain order. Large sections of the population strove for independence with a fanatical religious zeal. The Roman soldier, perhaps a blue-eyed veteran from Gaul, feared a knife in his ribs; the British Tommy might expect a bullet in his back. There were collaborationists; there were merchants who tried to do business with all parties; peaceful scholars and students whose only interest was cultural and religious. Among the subject population bitter and destructive debates went on concerning the best way to deal with the national problem. Most of the poor, as usual, suffered in silence.

The Temple was an important vested interest for a minority of priests. Herod the Great had kept the high-priesthood in his pocket, appointing obscure men who would do his will. After his death a few strong Sadducean families passed it around among themselves. Rome made sure of their loyalty by a simple expedient. The procurator kept the high priest's vestments locked up and let them out for ceremonial occasions. But the Sadducees, who are often thought to have been wealthy landowners, found their power and influence slipping. The common people flocked to the Pharisees, who were more conscious of popular needs and by their rulings on legal matters mitigated the hard lot of the working man. The high priests often had to bow to public opinion and follow Pharisaic rubrics in the Temple ritual.

The climate of Jerusalem is healthful, and usually pleasant and bracing. In the clear air, with the limestone hills all about him, many a modern pilgrim has found it easy to meditate on religious themes and to recall the presence of God. The city's inhabitants are apt to be hopeful and energetic. Many of them are genuinely religious, though perhaps the average man is no more pious than his counterpart elsewhere. But when droughts come and the cisterns are nearly empty, and the shirocco wind blows from the desert, people become anxious and irritable and tempers rise. It is a good time for the authorities to forbid public gatherings and for peaceful men to keep indoors. If, in addition, there have been incidents, a deep sense of foreboding pervades the city, and a man fears the passerby whom he meets in the streets. As in the last days of 1947, the routine of civilization stops. Each nation keeps to its own quarter, and few are daring enough to cross the no-man's-land between.

This is the city to which Jesus came. What he hoped to accomplish we cannot learn from his words but only guess from his actions; perhaps it was not so much that he had

a plan for Israel, as that he must speak. He rode into the
city on an ass, and this action may have been a symbolic
summons to the people to accept his leadership; Matthew
saw in it the fulfilment of the prophecy of Zechariah. At
the same time, it suggested a peaceful, not a violent, purpose. But would everyone understand it so? The prophecy
read, "Behold, thy king cometh, meek and sitting upon an
ass" (Zech. 9:9)—but what does a king do but reign?
He had often been addressed as Son of David. Now, as he
entered, the people took up the shout of the 118th Psalm,
with which they welcomed pilgrims to a festival; but they
added the words, "Blessed is the coming kingdom of our
father David," and some spread their garments for him
to ride over, just as Jehu's followers had done when that
bloody man was anointed king of Israel by a son of the
prophets.

Some time during this last visit Jesus also was anointed.
It happened in the house of Simon the Leper, when they
were sitting crosslegged on the floor eating out of a common dish: a woman came from behind and poured a
precious ointment on his head. The evangelist has added
a touching moral that suggests her love and devotion.
But the words of Jesus are revealing—"she has anointed
me for my burial." To be called king of Israel in these
days means almost certain death. Perhaps this explains
why Jesus could not deny it when the high priest asked
if he were the Anointed, the son of the Blessed. He had
been physically anointed; still more, he had been chosen
by God for leadership of the nation, even though he had
no intention of exercising political power. Whatever word
may be used to denote Jesus' activity in Jerusalem, our
gospels now show him in a messianic rôle, as religious
head of the Jewish commonwealth.

One of his first acts was the cleansing of the Temple. We know from rabbinical sources that there were complaints about the conditions under which sacrificial animals were sold. It may even be that inspectors did not approve a victim unless it had been purchased from the right people. Jesus drove out these hucksters, and in the confusion the tables of the money-changers were overturned. He refused to allow the Temple precincts to be made a short-cut for carrying vessels from one part of the city to another. Does this mean that his followers had temporary control of the Temple area?

The cleansing of the Temple was so dangerous and revolutionary a defiance that we can hardly imagine the gospel tradition inventing it. What did he hope to accomplish? Certainly he could not control the Temple for any length of time. It was probably a symbolic act such as the Old Testament prophets performed: his way of saying that God was coming to execute judgment on the priesthood, as Malachi predicted—perhaps had come, and was acting through Jesus. If the nation did not repent, God would visit the Temple with a still more severe condemnation. There is an old and persistent tradition that Jesus prophesied the destruction of the Temple; it was even said at the hearing before the high priest that he himself had threatened to destroy the Temple, but witnesses could not be found to substantiate this.

Mark has the story of the cursing of the fig tree. This may be the parable of Luke 13:6-9 made over into a miracle. A man comes seeking figs and wants to cut down the barren tree; but the gardener persuades him to try cultivating and manuring and to see if next year the tree will bear. Jerusalem is to have one more chance, but only one. The parable of the wicked husbandmen is to much the same effect. The landlord sends slaves to collect his revenues, and lastly his own son; when the son is killed, the lord himself comes to do judgment. The point is not so much that Jesus claims to be son of God, or that the tradition claims it for him; it is simply that this is the last chance.

It is curious, as we have remarked before, that according to the sources Jesus said nothing in Jerusalem about the Good News of the Kingdom of God and God's gracious seeking of sinners. He assumes that God is king and will assert his sovereignty, but it is altogether a message of judgment and the phrase "Kingdom of God" is not used. This may mean that Jewish society as a whole had already rejected his message, and there was no use proclaiming it except to the few who gathered around him, in Jerusalem as elsewhere. He had told his disciples, "Into whatever city you enter and they do not receive you, go out into the streets and say, 'The very dust which cleaves to us from your city we wipe off our feet against you; but know this, that the Kingdom of God has drawn near" (Luke 10:10-11). The woes once pronounced against Chorazin and Bethsaida are now spoken against Jerusalem.

If Jesus' activity in Jerusalem can be called a protest, it was against the way of the world—the cynical collaboration of the Sadducees and the violence of their opponents, the zealots. Both were leading the people to ruin. The very idea of the Kingdom of God was also an implicit condemnation of the Roman empire. The world's great commonwealth, even though it was more tolerable than the economic and political chaos it replaced, was based on human ambition, pride, greed and the worship of false gods more than on principles of justice and service to its inhabitants. It could be tolerated and obeyed but one who embraced the Kingdom of God could feel no warmth of patriotic allegiance toward it. Imperial taxes must be paid —Jesus raises no hand against the Roman eagles—but he goes no further. Man's ultimate allegiance is to the king-ship of God.

There was less to be said against the Pharisees. Jesus actually had much in common with them; but for all their genuine social concern, their program was too narrowly nationalistic and sectarian, it was too involved in trifles, and it did not get at the root of man's need. Only the way of Jesus could save Israel: his vivid consciousness of the reality and activity of God, his concentration on the few things needful, his bold love for enemies that builds up broken relationships and forms new ones. Reject this, and the end is in sight. God's Kingdom will surely come—there is no way to frustrate his will—but for those who reject that Kingdom there is only the outer darkness. It may have been Jesus' hope that by one last appeal, by one final warning of judgment, the nation could be saved. The warning was rejected except by the relatively small group which followed Jesus.

Those who supported the three centers of power and influence in Judaea—Rome, the high priesthood, the Phari-saic leadership—could not look with favor on Jesus' mes-sage. His authority and independence threatened them. All his sayings and actions indicate a magisterial certainty and confidence. His way of understanding the Old Testa-ment revelation did not fit easily into any of the usual systems of piety and law. If he had been a withdrawn and quiet hermit, cultivating his own inner life, or the leader of a small sect of perfectionists, he could have been toler-ated. As it was, he had broadcast his message and had a substantial popular following. The authorities feared such

a man, however gentle his methods had been. And Jesus
had cleansed the Temple.

Our sources tell that he was seized at night, in the place
called Gethsemane on the Mount of Olives, by a detachment of temple police, or at any rate armed servants of the
high priest. A disciple known to us as Judas Iscariot—
a name that may mean Judah of the village of Kerioth or
Judah the traitor—led them there and identified him. The
precautions taken were justified, for a follower of Jesus
wounded one of the captors. Our Lord was led to the
high priest's house, where a small group of members of the
Sanhedrin examined him. This must not be called a trial;
it conforms to none of the established legal procedures.
Most of those present must have been Sadducees. We have
no reason to suppose that Pharisees were involved. For their
own protection and that of the people generally, it had
been their policy to insist on public trials in proper form,
and they would not have condoned a secret night trial or
the judicial murder of an innocent man. The story that
came out of this hearing, as it passed into the tradition of
the Church, is that witnesses against Jesus did not agree
in their testimony, yet Jesus himself answered that he was
Messiah.

To be Messiah was no crime in Jewish Law, but in
Roman law it might be construed as treason or sedition.
At any rate, the police powers of a Roman governor were
broad enough that he could take action against any person
likely to disturb the peace. The actual trial took place
before Pilate in the morning—perhaps in the castle of the
Antonia, at the northwest corner of the Temple area, as
many archaeologists believe, or in the old royal palace in
the western part of the city, where Pilate may have had his

headquarters when he came down from Caesarea to Jerusalem.

One or two points in John's account of the trial have a ring of realism. Pilate is represented as convinced that Jesus was personally harmless. He seems also to have been conscious of Tiberius' colonial policy—the emperor wanted his provinces well governed and as happy and peaceful as possible, and Pilate wished to have no report reach his superior's ears that an innocent man had been condemned. At the same time, Tiberius had an almost paranoid fear of treason. The priestly leaders, knowing this, insisted that Jesus was a disturber of the *pax Romana*—"if you let this man go, you are no friend of the emperor"—and when this was said, Pilate had no recourse but to give the sentence "To the Cross." Once he had done this, he was in a stronger position. The placard which he had set on the Cross, "The King of the Jews," was offensive to Jewish sensibilities, and the leaders protested. "Write it this way," they asked, "He said, 'I am the King of the Jews.'" "What I have written, I have written," answered Pilate. In other words, "this is what we Romans will do to any King of the Jews."[1]

Jesus, then, was condemned by a Roman official in a Roman court, and executed by crucifixion—the Roman method of killing by torture, reserved for slaves and criminals of the lower classes. The responsibility for this rests primarily on Pilate; the priestly accusers must bear an almost equal share of the guilt; but there is no reason to attach blame to the Pharisees or the Jewish people as a whole.

He was handed over to the soldiers, who indulged what-

[1] A. T. Olmstead, *Jesus in the Light of History* (New York, 1942), pp. 229-37.

ever propensities they might have had for brutality and re-
venge. As usual, Jesus was expected to carry the heavy cross
beam which would be affixed to the pole or tree already
standing at the place of execution. Perhaps he was unable
to bear its weight. A Jew from Cyrene in north Africa
named Simon, evidently well known to later Christians as
the father of Alexander and Rufus, was pressed into service to carry the beam. We do not know the route of the
Via Dolorosa. If Pilate's praetorium was at the Antonia,
the traditional way of the Cross may approximately follow
it. Otherwise it led from the royal palace north and east
outside the city. The place Golgotha may have been where
tradition puts it, inside the present Church of the Holy
Sepulchre; or, if the second north wall of Jerusalem followed the line of the present wall, it was in what is now
the new city, not far from the Damascus Gate.

Once the Cross was ready, the condemned man was
nailed to it or tied to it by thongs. Death sometimes came
only after days of torture; it was caused by the cutting
off of circulation and the accompanying shock, gangrene
or other infections; heat, thirst and insects heightened the
misery of the dying gibbeted man. People sometimes, out of
mercy and pity, brought opiates; Jesus refused when sour
wine was offered him. That he died after only six hours—
or, as the later evangelists have it, three—was a marvellous
release. During his last hours he may have repeated verses
of the Psalms and meditated on them. The quotation,
"My God, my God, why hast thou forsaken me?"—spoken
in his native Aramaic, not the original Hebrew—shows that
he was spared none of the bitterness of human emotion.
The twenty-second Psalm ends on a note of triumph, and
to repeat it was an act of faith, a faith that goes beyond
despair and tragedy. God had not intervened to save him,

and by any human way of thinking his cause had failed; yet in trust he called upon God.

It was an act of piety to bury the dead, and a religious Jew saw to it that he was laid in a tomb—a new grave, since a criminal might not be buried with one's own family. The so-called Garden Tomb gives a good idea of the original appearance of the Holy Sepulchre, and other examples are at the Tombs of the Kings, where Queen Helena of Adiabene and her husband were buried. Here a large disc-shaped stone stood in a stone trough and could be rolled along to close the entrance of the rock-cut cave.

Jesus had come to Jerusalem prepared to die. He had already been under suspicion in Galilee, and he had no illusion about the danger and difficulty of his undertaking. The king he wanted for Israel was God himself, but Jesus was the one divinely appointed to bring the nation under the yoke of that Kingdom. If the people could be led to accept the way which our Lord saw so clearly, he would be successful, even if it meant his death. Burkitt has used the metaphor of a "forlorn hope." A detachment or task force does a particular job; it is wiped out, but as a result the battle is won. Yet even if this forlorn hope should fail, Jesus must do his duty—he must warn, while there is time —and, after all, the issue is in the hands of God.

Looked at from one side, as the murder of an innocent man, the Crucifixion of Jesus is a senseless crime, just as the slaughter of innocent people in all the world's wars from its beginning is senseless and abhorrent to God. The Cross gets its meaning from Jesus' obedience and faith, and from the Resurrection and all that followed. One cannot imagine the God whom Jesus preached demanding the blood of his Son and Messiah, or even the blood of one of his faithful prophets. All that such a God could ask of him would be his obedience, his loyalty, and his faith. That is what is asked of everyone, and it is the whole duty of man. This complete union with the will of God was what led to the death of Christ.

Christian faith looks at the Crucifixion from another side. In the words of the Apostle Paul, God was in Christ reconciling the world to himself—even and especially in the Crucifixion. This insight of St. Paul fits with the character of the Father God in the gospels. God, through the ministry of Jesus, reaches out to man to bring him back to himself. This is presupposed by the three parables of Luke 15 and by at least two of the parables of the Kingdom. God does not cease his outreach even when human sin leads to the Crucifixion.

Jesus' own attitude to his coming death is best understood from the story of the Last Supper. The studies of Joachim Jeremias make it all but certain that Mark is right in regarding this final meal as a Passover celebration.[2] Passover is a memorial of God's saving action at the time of the Exodus and it looks forward to the restoration of Israel in the Kingdom of God. The celebrant or head of the family at the paschal meal explains the meaning of the feast, and on this occasion Jesus added a new interpretation. When he broke the bread and offered the cup he connected them with the breaking of his body and the shedding of his blood.

The words and accompanying actions actually suggest that he expected, not crucifixion, but death by stoning, at the hands of the Sanhedrin or a Jewish mob, for crucifixion did not ordinarily involve the shedding of blood or the breaking of the body. However this may be, Jesus re-

---

[2] J. Jeremias, *The Eucharistic Words of Jesus* (New York, 1955), pp. 1-60.

garded his death as a sacrifice that would lead the way to fulfillment of the Passover hope. It would inaugurate the new Covenant, God's new way of dealing with men, which was the burden of his message in Galilee when he proclaimed the forgiveness of sins. Here in the Last Supper is the link between the teacher of Galilee and the Messiah of Jerusalem. This sacrifice would be "for many"—to the benefit of the whole people of God—and this was no strange or outlandish notion, for it was believed that the Maccabean martyrs had given their lives as a sacrifice for the benefit of the nation.

The Bible never conceals or minimizes the hideousness of evil. But the biblical writers believe that, once the evil is done, God can bring good out of it. He can use the wicked past as the point of departure for his triumphant activity in history. Jesus' attitude to his own death is the supreme example of this biblical doctrine.

His faith is itself a victory. But within forty-eight hours his disciples were confident that they had seen him alive and that he was with them as a living presence. There was to be no waiting for the general resurrection when all should rise, for God had already raised him up, and he was now more than the prophet of Galilee and the king whom they wanted in Jerusalem. He was reigning in heaven, and his messiahship was of a more transcendent sort than they could ever have imagined. From this point Christianity begins to emerge as a new universal religion, still closely united with Judaism but soon to go beyond it. And the whole story of Jesus and his teaching begins to be told in the light of the new faith.

CHAPTER XI

THE INCARNATION AND THE PROBLEM OF JESUS' INDIVIDUALITY

HISTORICAL study cannot satisfy all our curiosity about the life of Jesus, and yet he is not unknown to us. We are left with the picture of Jesus of Nazareth as a concrete, individual and convincing character against the background of first-century Palestinian Judaism. The question then arises how this picture is related to the Christ of Christian faith, who is described in the Nicene Creed as "God from God, light from light, true God from true God, begotten, not made, who for us and for our salvation came down from heaven . . . and was made man," and whom St. Paul describes with a more fertile poetic imagination, using every metaphor that comes to his mind to express Christ's saving activity. We cannot ignore the historical facts nor adjust them arbitrarily to fit the dogma. Indeed, if the dogma is tenable, it must not only fit the facts but be illuminated by them.

One question immediately arises. Can one who belongs so definitely to a time and place in history be at the same time universal and eternal?

It is no new question. To many in the early centuries of Christianity the particularity of Jesus was a scandal. Most Greek Christians accepted current philosophical ideas of God without question and combined them with the monotheism of the Old Testament. God, they believed, was happy, serene, unchangeable, incorporeal, incapable of suffering, and so on. In so far as the deity could be conceived of in human terms, he was Superman, like the gods of the Homeric pantheon. It cannot be denied that, however slightly, these ideas have affected the portrait of Christ in the Fourth Gospel. The docetists of the first and second centuries went so far as to say that Christ could only *appear* in human form, for he could not change, suffer or die. Certain gnostics eliminated the historical element almost entirely from their picture of Christ. In its place they put the myth of a Redeemer who comes down from the heavenly sphere and brings his own people—or rather their spirits—back to the realm of light from which in the first place they had fallen. The Redeemer's name was Christ, but almost any other name would have served as well.

Most Christians, by a sure instinct, resisted this tendency. Even though the Johannine writers are influenced by it, they combat it. Ignatius of Antioch shows only slight knowledge of the human story of Jesus but insists that he came in the flesh; Ignatius could think of no more powerful way to emphasize his true humanity. The synoptic gospels and the testimony of Paul continued to guarantee the genuinely historic and concrete character of the revelation and redemption in Christ. Nicene orthodoxy, while asserting Christ's unity of essence with the godhead, maintained the historical and human linkage. But the heresies of Apollinarianism and Monophysitism show how hard it was for Greek thinkers to take history seriously. Starting with a dogmatic, prefabricated doctrine of God, they sought to force Christ into it. And even when the matter was apparently settled at Chalcedon, there remained Cyril of Alexandria's doctrine of the impersonal

humanity of Jesus. As a theory it may be defensible—
Christ must somehow represent and redeem *all* humanity,
he is not merely one individual among many—but the
doctrine too easily slips into the notion that everything
significant about Jesus comes from his divine nature, not
the individual Jewish first-century humanity that learned
and prayed and lived and died. One cannot escape the judgment that much popular teaching and piety, in medieval
and modern times, ignores most of what makes Jesus'
humanity significant. When this happens, he has become,
to all intents and purposes, a symbol and little else.

The modern attempt to recover the story of Jesus posed
the problem once more. Confronted by it, not a few
adopted a Unitarian theology. Others have found this
solution unnecessary, superficial and unsatisfying, and
accordingly orthodox theologians, in Protestantism at least,
take the doctrine of Christ's humanity and divinity with
full seriousness. As they understand orthodoxy, everything
that Christ did he did as both man and God, and no separation can be made between the activities of his two natures.
Donald Baillie remarks that, outside the Roman Church,
docetism is dead.[1] At the same time, the human mind is
always prone to oversimplify theological and philosophical
problems, and it takes some imagination to keep the ideas
of Jesus' divinity and humanity together. The recent emphasis on the *kerygma* or proclamation material of the
gospels rather than their *didache* or moral teaching, the
preoccupation with Pauline and Johannine faith as the
essence of the New Testament religion, could lead once
again to neglect of the concrete historical reality of Jesus'
life and particularly his teaching.

Surely nothing less than the historic Christian faith will

[1] D. M. Baillie, *God Was in Christ* (New York, 1948), pp. 9-20.

permanently satisfy those who read and ponder the Bible and are moved by it. Without this faith, Jesus is no more than one among many, however great an emotional appeal he makes, and it is hard to see why he should be the norm for our religious life rather than the Jewish Law or some philosophy—or, for that matter, the type of mysticism that dispenses with historical religion altogether. Without Christian faith our ethical and spiritual standards are relative. On the other hand, the Christian faith makes no sense unless the Christ who is proclaimed has an individuality that can be identified. If he is no more than a redeemer-symbol, he can be used as a convenient mold into which one may pour any systematic doctrine one chooses—Platonism or Thomism or Calvinism.[2]

The doctrine of Incarnation is not that God masqueraded as man, nor that Christ had a human body and a divine mind, nor that he was a middle term between God and man but neither one nor the other completely, nor yet that he was a human hero promoted to the rank of godhead. It is rather that the humanity of Jesus of Nazareth was completely united with God, and that everything he did and said as man was at the same time the word and activity of God. This presupposes that in the Incarnate Lord God's attributes were in some way limited; in so far as God is unlimited he condescended to lay aside that aspect of his deity; yet all of God that can be expressed in humanity is here manifest.[3]

[2] One might object that we are doing what Paul repudiates—"knowing Christ-after-the-flesh" or "knowing-after-the-flesh Christ." But when Paul says this, he does not mean that the story of Christ's life is no consequence—he himself shows knowledge of Jesus' human character—he means only that we must not know Christ externally, without faith, or judge him by secular standards.

[3] Donald Baillie works this out in some detail in his book *God Was in Christ.*

If we take the historic Christian faith and the teaching of the New Testament seriously, we have in the synoptic gospels the most specific and concrete revelation of God that has ever been given to man. The revelation comes in two forms in the gospels. We know God as the God whom Jesus worshipped and of whom he spoke; we know him also as the God whose activity is manifested in Jesus' own life and work. The two methods of revelation cannot be distinguished except in theory, and this God is clearly recognizable as the one proclaimed by the Old Testament prophets—all-powerful, all-righteous, all-loving. Jesus adds no formal teaching about God to what was already known in Judaism; he takes for granted what we call ethical monotheism. What he added was a vivid and passionate awareness of God—not so much a *feeling* of his presence, for he often pictures God as the master who is away on a journey and may return at any moment—but rather a profound and practical conviction that God is alive and active, which controls every thought that he thinks and every action he undertakes. So far as we can tell from his teaching, he knows God by faith—as did the prophets and as we ourselves do.

At the same time, Jesus brings certain features of God's character into high relief. What is most striking is that, as seen in Jesus, he is so little concerned for his glory and his renown. Not only does Jesus show scant interest in the question of his own relation to God—which is for us, and rightly, one of the most important issues of our lives— God himself asks love and filial fidelity more than monarchical worship and awe. God's power and majesty are never questioned—the very phrase "Kingdom of God" indicates this—but Jesus never finds it necessary to exhort men to worship God, just as he never satisfies our curiosity about his own relationship to the Father. To know God intimately is to see more than his power and glory. As one of the rabbis said, "Wherever scripture mentions the greatness of God, there mention is also found of his humility." Or, to put it differently, his supreme glory is his grace; he is glorified most truly when he is loved by forgiven sinners. Anyone who reads the Old Testament realizes that Jesus was not the first to teach the fatherhood of God, but with him it is a controlling idea, always in the forefront of his consciousness.

God, according to Jesus, takes the initiative in seeking and saving that which was lost, and Jesus himself follows this pattern of activity. Montefiore remarked that here a new note comes into Judaism; while the Pharisees believed in repentance and welcomed the repentant sinner, they expected him to make the first move, and they themselves kept aloof from wrongdoers and their defilement. Now it must be acknowledged that the idea of a seeking and saving God is not absent from the Old Testament—the prophecy of Hosea furnishes a good example—but here his saving initiative is concretely shown. Jesus does not hold aloof from sinners, and he has no fear of defilement, ceremonial or moral; he seems to regard the power of holiness and righteousness as incomparably greater. The essence of Jesus' message is the Kingdom of God which reaches out and gathers men into itself.

At the same time, he executes judgment on the oral law, the ministry, the Temple, and even the Chosen People themselves. It would almost appear that Jesus feels little responsibility for the institutions which go to make up so much of man's life, yet his denunciations are made with a heavy heart. It is a tragedy when even a barren fig tree must be cut down. The fact is, however, that no institution can take the place of God. He has made institutions and he can replace them. God has slight interest in them as such; they have value only as they do his work and minister to his people.

Jesus in his teaching often pictures God as doing the unexpected and arresting thing—the ways of God are not those of men—and Jesus himself behaves in the same way. No respecter of persons, he frequently takes the part of the poor, the unrespectable, and the sinful.

Finally, Jesus dies on the Cross rather than be untrue to his principles or choose another and less dangerous scene of activity. He gives himself to his people, as he had given himself all through his ministry, by refusing to desert his post and advancing to Jerusalem. This also corresponds to something in the character of God—though we be faithless, he remains faithful—and even the thought of his going down into and sharing suffering and death, difficult though it may be to conceive, is like the passionate yearning and deep involvement which he manifests in some of the words of the Old Testament prophets.

We have spoken of all this as a revelation of God, but it is more than revelation in the sense of imparting facts or truth; it is God in action, performing what he reveals of his own character.

Although the picture of Jesus in the gospels is concrete and specific, at the same time it has the element of universality. Jesus is not merely the product of his own time and people. We have indicated that at many points he repeats and emphasizes what was already known of God in the Old Testament. But, more than this, we see one who is born a Jew and loyal to his own people and their religion transcending the boundaries of Judaism. He does not deal with other men as Jews or Gentiles but as human beings, and his religious judgments are not limited by Jewish tradition; they are on the basis of a universal monotheistic faith.

In previous chapters we have already asked whether Jesus' teaching may not be limited at one point by his outlook as a first-century Galilean Jew. His apparent lack of concern for social order can be put down to his prophetic judgment on human institutions. Human beings must find the true meaning of their lives as members of a family, and any social order which depersonalizes them and makes them mere units is doomed to destruction. If, however, Jesus had known that in future centuries society would become more and more complex and interrelated, beyond the power of human imagination to comprehend, what would he have said to his followers as they wrestle with the problem of their responsibilities as citizens? Would he have said, "Save yourselves from this wicked and perverse generation"?—in other words, "Be just and forgiving in your personal relationships, for nothing can save the social organization as a whole"? This is possible. He might, however, have bade them do what the early Christians did, i.e. create a society of their own within the larger society, in which life could have more meaning, although as culture becomes complex and the state more powerful this course is increasingly difficult to follow. It is also possible that he might have encouraged them to bring the values of the Kingdom of God—deep personal relationships, forgiveness and non-resistance—into the society from which they could not escape. No one can tell what he might have said, and there seems no way to answer the question except through the experimental activity of Christians. Christians themselves may find a way to arrest the depersonalization of life and the fragmentation of culture through the revival of the Church and active participation in the various concerns of society. Jesus' teaching of the Kingdom of God is, after all, universal in its appeal. Whatever means we may take to prepare ourselves and our fellow Christians for it, it remains as a permanent hope and a judgment on human institutions.

The question of Jesus' uniqueness and universality is also raised in a curious way by the Jewish movement known as hasidism, which arose in Poland in the eighteenth century and of which Martin Buber is the most distinguished present-day exponent.[4] A Christian who for the first time reads the sayings of the Baal-shem-tov and his hasidic followers realizes with something of a shock that they possess some of the quality of the teachings of Jesus. The same spirit was, of course, found here and there in certain rabbis of the first and second centuries, particularly those who are quoted in the Pirqe Aboth or Sayings of the Fathers, in the Mishnah. Like Jesus, the hasidim of modern times went to the despised irreligious masses, with a message of religious joy and the love of God. They sought to break down the barrier between the people and the rabbis. Their ideal was not a separated expert clergy but the simple believing man. Faith and grace, rather than legal observance, were the center of their piety. Their purpose was to transform the lives of men and thereby society and the world. The simple everyday things of life were to be hallowed. Their leader, the Baal-shem-tov, was humble, like Jesus, and attracted men to himself in a similar way. "Whoever has heard him," says Buber, "feels that the speech is directed at him." Hasidism has a Messianic background which even includes the idea of a decisive conflict between the forces of evil and those of the Kingdom of God.

[4] M. Buber, *Hasidism* (New York, 1948).

There are, however, significant differences. Hasidism is in one way a highly sophisticated religion with a complicated philosophical background. Many of its ideas come out of the esoteric mediaeval Jewish movement which we call kabbalism and may ultimately have originated in gnosticism. Hasidism is based on centuries-old speculations about the evil impulse in man, and it is frankly mystical, as the gospel tradition is not. Love, in hasidism, appears to be much more emotional and self-conscious than in the teachings of Jesus. Part of the difference is the difference between the mediaeval ghetto and first-century Palestine. Hasidism puts much emphasis on spiritual direction of the masses, with its attendant danger of domination. The movement is entirely world-affirming and lacks the element of renunciation and sacrifice which is found in Jesus' teaching. The Messianic age is believed to come gradually as the result of hasidic redemption. Finally, of course, the Baal-shem-tov is not an absolute figure as Jesus is for Christians; he is simply the first and greatest of a line of spiritual leaders.

One can say, of course, that the elements of hasidism which remind us of the teaching of Jesus are implicit in the Old Testament and in first-century Judaism, so that when the favorable historical and psychological situation arises they reappear. Hasidism thus bears witness to the spiritual needs of mankind.

A Christian may, however, see still more. Hasidism may be one way in which the spirit of Christ comes to men when all other avenues seem to be closed to his approach. The essence of Christ's message is that God is a seeking and saving God who, although he is ignored by the wise and prudent, reveals himself to babes. The theological matrix in which hasidism appears is not the most significant thing about it; what is significant is the message of God's grace which can be apprehended by faith and is made perfect in love. Likewise, the Gentile idea of redemption which in the Creeds interprets the coming of Christ is not significant in itself—what is significant is the character of God the Redeemer, and this is seen most perfectly in the life of Jesus. There have been many times when Christian theology has been presented as only a redemption-pattern and the character of the human Jesus was forgotten. On the other hand, Judaism in the eighteenth century unexpectedly produced human beings who in significant ways remind us of this same Jesus. This may serve to warn us that Christian theology must never forget the rock from which it was hewn, and this is the Old Testament and first-century Judaism.

But why was there a redemption-pattern? Why do the Creeds, and the New Testament itself use language that is so foreign to present-day historical and scientific thought? Is there any value in the traditional Christian formulations?

Few questions are more vigorously debated by students of the New Testament. In early Christian writings the universe is thought of as consisting of three layers—heaven, earth and hell or Gehenna. The world contains not only God and human beings, animals and plants, but angels and demons as well. History is not, as we usually think of it, a continuous process in which a variety of causes is at work, but a drama of perdition and redemption. In this drama the world's history is divided into three parts. The first covers all events until the coming of Christ, and all this period is looked upon as a preparation for the time of salvation. The ministry of Christ, climaxed by his death and resurrection, inaugurates a new age, for he has tri-

umphed over the forces of evil. Christians are now living
in a time of expectation, for although the decisive battle
has occurred, the complete establishment of the Kingdom
of God is not yet. The final age will come when the Son of
Man returns in glory to judge the world, a permanent time
of bliss when nothing any longer resists God's will. But
meanwhile the Christian experiences the joy of the new age,
and is in some sense a transformed person. In baptism he
is initiated into the new fellowship, and the Lord's Supper
gathers up for the worshipping community the memory of
past redemption and the hope of future glory, presenting
these as accomplished facts and bringing them into present
experience.

The debate revolves around two questions. Which elements of this pattern—angels and demons, for example—
are less important and can be eliminated without danger
to the values of Christian faith? And to what extent can
the whole pattern be reinterpreted in the language of modern philosophy?

For many the problem does not exist at all; they can
initiate themselves into the biblical language and appreciate
the values of the pattern, discarding or reinterpreting certain elements by a kind of religious instinct. For example,
few believers are disturbed by the fact that in the Coper-
nican universe there is no up or down; Jesus at his ascension
did not have to "go up" into the sky, he returned to the
spiritual realm where God is. But others find more of a
stumbling-block in the older language, and if they are to
find a satisfying faith they must come to terms with the
difficulties of the redemption-pattern.

Patterns of sacred story are as old as religion, and it
may be helpful to compare the Christian story with an
older formulation. Theodor Gaster's *Thespis* is a recent

attempt to see a pattern of myth, ritual and sacred drama underlying the Canaanite texts from Ras Shamra, various Egyptian, Babylonian and Hittite ceremonies, and the *Bacchae* of Euripides.[5] First come rites of penitence and purgation culminating in the death of the god in a ritual combat, then the god's resurrection and enthronement which lead to new life and the revival of reproductive powers for the earth and the worshipping community, and, lastly, a period of jubilation. Gaster argues that many Old Testament psalms reflect parts of this pattern. He might have given parts of the Pauline epistles and the Book of Revelation as additional examples.

The Old Testament and the New have, however, sloughed off the unmoral elements of this old pattern if they have used it at all. The myth of the death and rebirth of vegetation and animal life, and the connection of this with the summer and winter solstices, have been left behind. Ancient man could not escape the idea of a combat between light and darkness and the succession of death and resurrection. What has happened in early Christianity is that this pattern, which expresses the aspirations and longings of humanity, is entirely recast. Now the ethical God of the Old Testament, who is all-righteous and all-loving, comes into human life in the person and ministry of Jesus, conquers the forces of evil which put him to death, and completes the story of the Cross with a triumphant resurrection. The divine combat has to do, not with the seasons and vegetation, but with moral and spiritual struggle in the life of man. Jesus himself first wins the fight against temptation by refusing to be deflected from his purpose. He rejects easy ways to leadership and political power and stands fast in the face of rejection and death. Thus he

---

[5] Theodor H. Gaster, *Thespis* (New York, 1950).

insures that his followers will be victorious in their own struggle and participate in his resurrection.

Another difference is that the Christian story, unlike the old myths, is firmly fixed in history. In this Christianity is like other religions of Semitic monotheism, Judaism and Islam. The Exodus and the prophetic ministry of Mohammed actually occurred. Thus the Christian story is not a myth in the classical sense of the word. From our sources we can isolate a core of hard fact, consistent within itself, and capable of being included in a scientific historical account. Surrounding this is an historical penumbra—a number of incidents that may well have occurred, that most Christians believe did occur, but which we cannot verify by ordinary historical methods. If they happened they are historical, but a judgment as to their historicity is always made on the basis of faith. Such are some of the miracles of Jesus, and of course his resurrection. It is a solid historical fact that the earliest disciples believed they had seen the risen Christ, but only faith can say that they were right in their belief.

A third part of the Christian story is entirely beyond history. When Paul, in Phil. 2:5-11, says that Christ existed originally in the nature of God, divested himself of his divine attributes and became man, and then that after his crucifixion God exalted him and gave him a name which is above every name, he is speaking of something no one could have directly experienced. This is a pure example of revelation and faith. Here Christianity expresses itself in what is usually called myth, that is, sacred story. It cannot be made subject to criticism, it can only be accepted or rejected.

The question so vigorously debated just now is whether this kind of imaginative picture is an essential part of

Christianity. My conviction is that the Christian Church cannot dispense with it, since religion is more than theology, philosophy and ethics, and the world view of a religion has to be expressed in its own particular language, which is akin to poetry but more than poetry. Believing intellectuals generally wish to understand their religion as fully as possible, and not merely to practice it, and therefore there will always be theology; and one of the aims of theology is to translate the language of faith into philosophical terms understandable to believer and unbeliever alike. While some believers dislike the prose of theology, it is for others a way of initiation into the language of faith.

We have already said that the Christian story is rooted in history. This is more than just a guarantee that it is not merely a construction of the religious imagination. It means, as well, that it is in a particular context. We can see this if we compare the crucifixion of Jesus with the death of another historical character, the Pawnee hero Petalesharoo. Petalesharoo determined to put an end to the custom of human sacrifice, and so, when a maiden was about to be slain, he substituted himself for the victim.[6] Let us say at once that, like the death of Socrates, this is for the benefit of others. It is a vicarious sacrifice, it is not in vain, and it is a kind of redemption. History knows of many such examples, and they are a sign that the principle behind the death of Jesus Christ is necessary for human society so long as any evil remains in the world. This is true even if in the deed of a man like Socrates there are elements of stubbornness and intellectual pride. But Petalesharoo's deed, and that of Socrates, do not have all the consequences of Jesus' sacrifice, nor do they have precisely the same

[6] Robert Redfield, *The Primitive World and Its Transformations* (Ithaca, N. Y., 1953), pp. 130-33.

meaning. To Christians the death of Jesus is an event that transforms all history.

One reason why this is so is that it is in a unique historical context. It is the climax of a ministry of outreach, self-giving, union with the will of God, and proclamation of a new order of things. If Jesus had not been, at one and the same time, the announcer of the Kingdom of God, a teacher in whom the unresolved issues of Judaism found an answer, and, finally, one who continued his prophetic work and his performance of God's will in the face of death, one may question whether the early Christians would have placed the same valuation on his life and death. As Christians look at it, he seems to have met a very definite situation and to have come at the fulness of time, when the prophets, wise men and scribes had prepared the way, and when the world, both Jewish and Graeco-Roman, was at least partly ready to understand and receive the new message. The pattern disclosed by Gaster's *Thespis* was not the only redemption-pattern current in the religious world. Many Greeks and orientals had a theology according to which a Redeemer taught the way of salvation to his chosen ones and so enabled them, or rather the divine spark in them, to rise to heaven and unite itself with the godhead. This Gnosis, as it was called, was extremely dangerous to Christianity, and many gnostics tried to dissolve the new religion into this non-historical mythical philosophy. But the very existence of Gnosis discloses a way prepared for the Christian story.

The Jew or Greek who gave his allegiance to Jesus could not avoid believing that his Messiah and Lord was universal and eternal in his significance. Therefore, he expressed his faith in terms that were not unrelated to theologies already in existence. But in one way the new

Christian faith was different from all others. Though its fundamental affirmation was a matter of faith, not historical or philosophical proof, it was an interpretation of an actual historical person much of whose teaching and activity was remembered and recorded. The gospel tradition prevented the new religion from becoming purely mythical. It also helped to preserve the connection of Christianity with the Hebrew religion and to provide a point of view by which to read the Old Testament. For the God whom Jesus worshipped and whose activity is manifest in his life is clearly recognizable as the God whom the prophets and psalmists served. He is no longer thought of as in any way national or racial, and his Law is purged of transitory and external features. The heart of the Old Testament message is expressed in the teaching of Jesus, and in his ministry we have the supreme example of the activity of God in history. The story of the gospels can be summed up in the words of Paul: "God was in Christ reconciling the world to himself . . . and he has committed to us the word of reconciliation."

GOOD descriptions of Galilee can be found in E. G. Kraeling, *Rand McNally Bible Atlas* (Chicago, 1956) and Sir George Adam Smith, *The Historical Geography of the Holy Land*, 20th ed. (London, n.d.), chaps. xx-xxi. On the history see also R. H. Pfeiffer, *History of New Testament Times with an introduction to the Apocrypha* (New York, 1949) and E. W. G. Masterman, *Studies in Galilee* (Chicago, 1909).

Indispensable for the Jewish background are G. F. Moore, *Judaism*, 3 vols. (Cambridge, Mass., 1927-30) and Louis Finkelstein, *The Pharisees*, 2 vols. (Philadelphia, 1938). S. W. Baron and J. L. Blau, *Judaism: Postbiblical and Talmudic Period* (New York, 1954) is a good brief source book. Leo Baeck, *The Pharisees* (New York, 1947) consists of interpretative essays.

I have written an article on "Jesus and First Century Galilee" in the volume *In Memoriam Ernst Lohmeyer*, ed. by W. Schmauch (Stuttgart, 1951). L. E. Elliott-Binns, *Galilean Christianity* (Chicago, 1956) sums up what we know about a very obscure subject.

Literature on the Dead Sea Scrolls has reached immense proportions. The most convenient translation of the main writings is T. H. Gaster, *The Dead Sea Scriptures* (New York, 1956). The most generally satisfactory summaries of knowledge are Millar Burrows, *The Dead Sea Scrolls*, New York, 1955), G. Vermès, *Discovery in the Judean Desert* (New York, 1956), and J. M. Allegro, *The Dead Sea Scrolls* (Harmondsworth, 1956), all containing select bibliographies. One should specially note D. Barthélemy and J. T. Milik, *Discoveries in the Judaean Desert I: Qumran Cave I* (Oxford, 1955) and *Revue Biblique*, LXIII (1956), 49-67. Certain matters mentioned in chaps. iv and v of the present work are discussed in more detail in my articles, "The Dead Sea Manual of Discipline and the Jerusalem Church of Acts," *Zeitschrift für die alttestamentliche Wissenschaft*, LXVI (1954), 106-20, and "Paul and the Manual of Discipline," *Harvard Theological Review*, XLVIII (1955), 157-65.

There are many biographies of Jesus which are useful in one way or another, such as those of Joseph Klausner, S. J. Case, Maurice Goguel, Edgar J. Goodspeed, Martin Dibelius, Rudolf Bultmann, A. T. Olmstead and B. W. Bacon. I have also found particularly helpful H. J. Cadbury, *The Peril of Modernizing Jesus* (New York,

1937); B. H. Branscomb, *Jesus and the Law of Moses* (New York, 1930); and C. G. Montefiore, *The Synoptic Gospels*, 2nd ed., 2 vols. (London, 1927). E. R. Goodenough's monumental work, *Jewish Symbols in the Greco-Roman Period*, 4 vols. (New York, 1953-54) is necessary for understanding the culture in which Jesus lived. See also Morton Smith, "Palestinian Judaism in the First Century" in Moshe Davis, ed., *Israel: Its role in Civilization* (New York, 1956), pp. 67-81.

For further reading on the subject of chap. vii, "Jesus and the Revolutionists," one may suggest W. R. Farmer, *Maccabees, Zealots and Josephus* (New York, 1956) and E. J. Bickerman, "The Historical Foundations of Postbiblical Judaism," in L. Finkelstein, ed., *The Jews: Their History, Culture and Religion* (New York, 1949).

There are many books on Jesus' teaching about the Kingdom of God, for example, F. C. Grant, *The Gospel of the Kingdom* (New York, 1940); R. Otto, *The Kingdom of God and the Son of Man* (Grand Rapids, Mich., n.d.); and H. B. Sharman, *Son of Man and Kingdom of God* (New York, 1943).

John Knox, *Christ the Lord* (Chicago, 1945) is a good introduction to the beginnings of Christology. The problem of myth is discussed in A. N. Wilder, *New Testament Faith for Today* (New York, 1955) and my article, "Rudolf Bultmann and the Mythology of the New Testament," *Anglican Theological Review*, XXXVI (1954), 29-47. Both of these cite much of the recent literature.

INDEX